101 Classic Homes of the Twenties

Floor Plans and Photographs

Harris, McHenry & Baker Co.

DOVER PUBLICATIONS, INC.

Mineola, New York

Published in Canada by General Publishing Company, Ltd., 30 Lesmill Road, Don Mills, Toronto, Ontario.

Bibliographical Note

This Dover edition, first published in 1999, is an unabridged republication of the work originally published in 1925 by Harris, McHenry & Baker Co., Elmira, New York, under the title *Better Homes at Lower Cost*.

Library of Congress Cataloging-in-Publication Data

Better homes at lower cost.
   101 classic homes of the twenties : floor plans and photographs / Harris, McHenry & Baker Co.
         p.   cm.
   Originally published: Better homes at lower cost. Elmira, N.Y. : Harris, McHenry & Baker Co., 1925.
   Includes index.
   ISBN 0-486-40731-4
   1. Suburban homes—United States Designs and plans. 2. Architecture, Domestic—United States Designs and plans. I. Harris, McHenry & Baker Co. II. Title.
NA7571.B38   1999
728'.37'097309042—dc21   99-15551
                                                                                CIP

Manufactured in the United States of America
Dover Publications, Inc., 31 East 2nd Street, Mineola, N.Y. 11501

Index

	Page		Page		Page		Page
Arden	16	Edenton	53	Kendall	32	Radcliff	65
Auburn	91	Elon	52	Kingston	75	Raeford	55
Avon	81	Elsworth	76			Regent	28
		Elwood	101	La Salle	38	Richmond	21
Belmont	18	Englewood	70	Lauder	104	Rosemary	103
Belvedere	45	Euclid	37	Lewiston	34		
Berkeley	7			Lincoln	48	San Lois	64
Brewster	88	Fairmont	97	Loraine	54	Somerset	29
Bristol	49	Fernwood	82	Luverne	57	Stoddard	36
Brookline	77	Forrest	102	Lynnhaven	85	Stoneleigh	66
Brownlee	59	Franklin	20			Stratford	14
Brunswick	43	Fremont	83	Manchester	27	Strathmore	44
Burnette	94			Marden	8		
		Garland	79	Marlowe	80	Tennyson	11
Cardenas	63	Genessee	78	Maryland	35	Thorndyke	67
Carlyle	10	Glendale	33	Mayfield	86	Thurston	50
Chelton	71	Glen Rae	92	Milton	30		
Chesterfield	23	Gordon	89	Monte Cristo	61	Van Buren	6
Cleveland	24	Grayling	72	Morgan	47	Varina	56
Clifton	98					Vernon	69
Collingwood	4	Hamilton	13	Norfolk	39	Victoria	31
Cornell	62	Hawthorn	60	Northcliff	5		
Crescent	96	Hazelwood	87			Washington	19
		Herndon	74	Oakdale	90	Warren	93
Dayton	100			Olive	84	Wayne	99
Devonshire	58	Irving	95	Olympia	42	Webster	9
Don Carlo	15			Oxford	40	Westhaven	17
Dumont	12	Jefferson	25			Westmoreland	22
Dumont Four	26	Jerome	46	Parkwood	73	Windsor	41
		Jewell	68	Preston	51		

Ask for an approximate cost sheet, also free contract forms

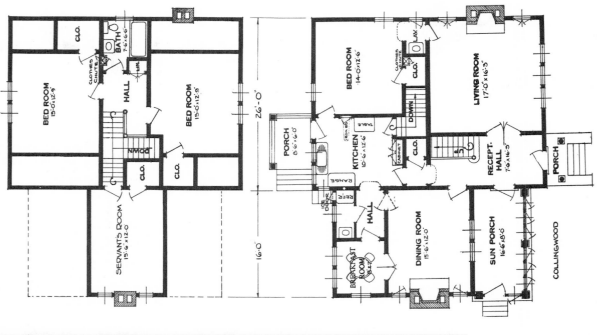

The COLLINGWOOD (Size 42x34')

It is appreciation that humanity really is seeking and not gold. Gold, gained honestly or dishonestly, is in turn paid for appreciation and applause. He is most appreciated by friend and neighbor who contributes to his community a substantial home of The Collingwood design, and unselfishly shares his comforts and pleasures with those of his kind.

4

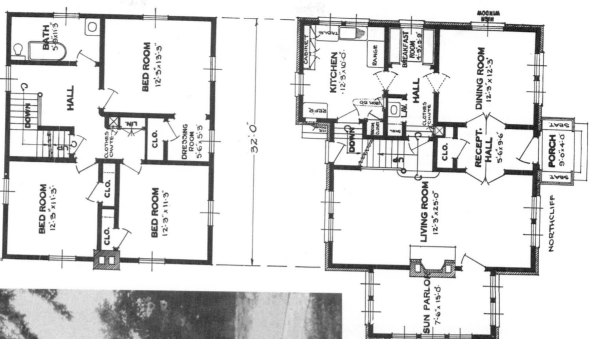

The first step toward home ownership is to secure a set of plans so that correct cost estimates may be made.

The NORTHCLIFF (Size 32x26′)

Every movement for human betterment first finds expression in the home. There is something in the inner being of optimistic men and women which prompts them to lend a hand to the helpless and give a word of cheer to the cheerless. Those who make The Northcliff their home will be prompted daily to radiate the sunshine its comforts will bring.

5

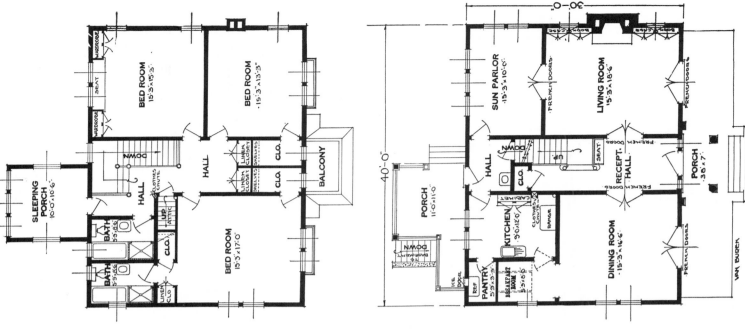

The VAN BUREN (Size 40x30')

Clean men, both of hand and heart, are invariably the product of happy home unions. It is around the harmonious hearthstone where the glow of mutual interest and understanding temper the finer senses that men mould character of sterling worth. It would be a violation of a natural law if homes in The Van Buren class should produce other than men of clean purpose.

6

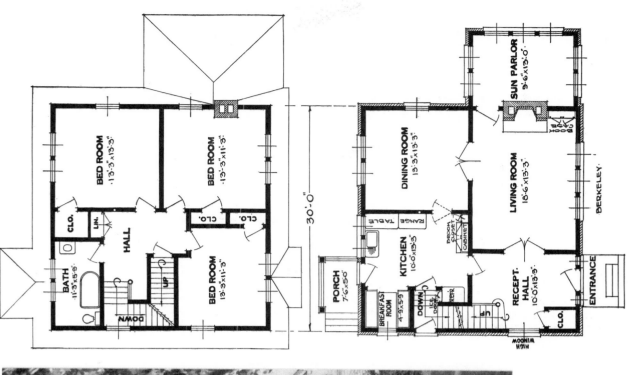

Second floor plan:
- BED ROOM 13'-3"x13'-3"
- BED ROOM 13'-3"x11'-3"
- BED ROOM 13'-3"x11'-3"
- CLO.
- LIN.
- CLO.
- CLO.
- HALL
- BATH 11'-3"x5'-9"
- UP
- DOWN
- 30'-0"

First floor plan:
- SUN PARLOR 9'-6"x13'-6"
- BOOK CASE
- DINING ROOM 13'-3"x13'-3"
- LIVING ROOM 16'-6"x13'-3"
- RANGE TABLE
- BROOM CLOSET
- CABINET
- KITCHEN 10'-0"x13'-3"
- PORCH 7'-6"x5'-0"
- BREAKFAST ROOM 4'-9"x5'-9"
- DOWN
- UP
- RECEPT. HALL 10'-0"x13'-5"
- CLO.
- ENTRANCE
- BERKELEY

The BERKELEY (Size 30x28')

It is around the fireside of happy homes where children chatter with glee and loving mothers watch over them with divine care that the best and noblest thoughts of men are generated. The germs of selfishness, envy and greed have little chance to multiply in homes of the substantial character of The Berkeley. From such homes come men quick of thought and fair of judgment.

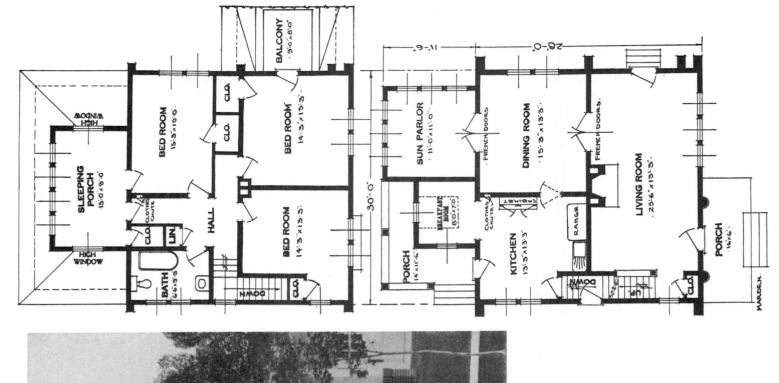

The MARDEN (Size 30x28')

All mothers should be free from those things which disturb and distress. They should at all times feel a sense of restfulness, serenity, peace and poise. Conditions for such a state of mind cannot be found in crowded districts, but rather in ideal private homes, in The Marden class, where only those influences are permitted which tend to satisfy and soothe the maternal senses.

8

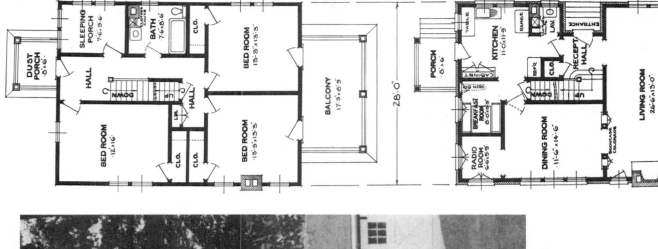

The WEBSTER (Size 28x36')

Those only are great who love and are kind, and these greatest of human faculties are best developed in the home. Those who strive hardest to attain a home, strive hardest for the development of the best in themselves and in turn bring out the best in others they meet. Striving for a home such as The Webster elevates, educates and ennobles.

9

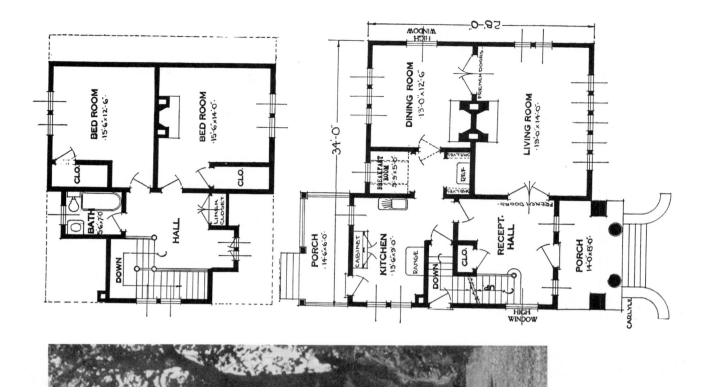

Floor plan labels — Second floor:
- BED ROOM 15'-6"x12'-6"
- BED ROOM 15'-6"x14'-0"
- CLO.
- CLO.
- BATH 5'-6"x7'-0"
- HALL
- LINEN CLOSET
- DOWN

Floor plan labels — First floor:
- DINING ROOM 13'-0"x12'-6"
- LIVING ROOM 13'-0"x14'-0"
- HIGH WINDOW
- FRENCH DOORS
- SHELVES
- REF.
- SHELVES
- BREAKFAST ROOM 8'-9"x5'-6"
- PORCH 14'-6"x6'-0"
- KITCHEN 13'-6"x9'-0"
- CABINET
- RANGE
- CLO.
- RECEPT. HALL
- DOWN
- UP
- FRENCH DOORS
- PORCH 14'-0"x8'-0"
- HIGH WINDOW
- CARLYLE
- 28'-0"
- 34'-0"

The CARLYLE (Size 34x28')

Humanity's earnest call is for kindness and good cheer. Those best fitted to do their bit toward human betterment are those who practice in their homes the principles which they endeavor to demonstrate abroad. Living up to one's moral standards is not a great task if the surroundings are satisfying and the arrangement of the home is as ideal as The Carlyle.

10

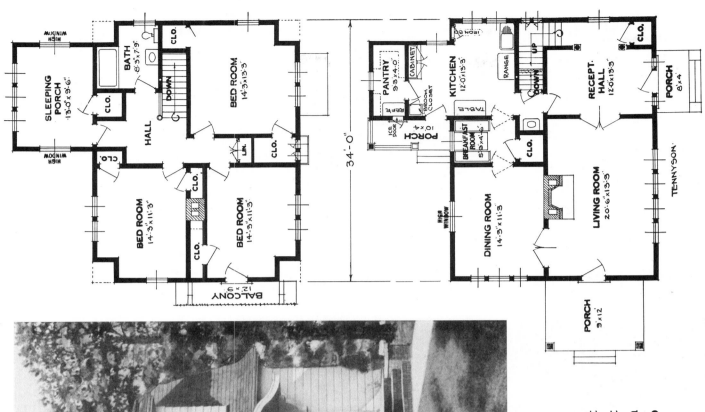

The TENNYSON (Size 34x26')

Love is the great heart opener, the great mind opener and developer. It enriches the life and lightens the heaviest burdens. It sweetens the hardest labor and makes self-sacrifice a joy. In beautiful new homes like The Tennyson there are no enemies of love—if the lesson has been learned that companionship is the price of peace.

11

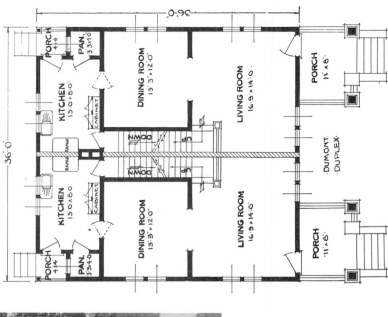

The DUMONT DUPLEX (Size 36x36')

The Dumont cannot be surpassed as a double house, and will make homes of exceptional advantages and refinements for those whose experience and education have taught them the value of good fellowship and neighborly kindness. Learning to co-operate with our fellow creatures is the secret of overcoming selfishness and all of its poisoning effects upon our better selves.

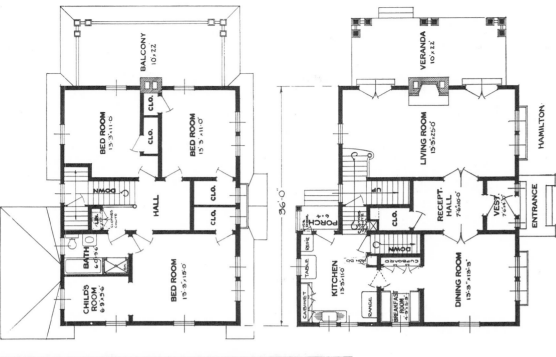

It cannot be estimated what civilization owes to pure-minded women who love their homes.

The HAMILTON (Size 36x26')

Nothing so stimulates and elevates a man as for his companion to believe in him, and in no other way can a man show his appreciation of such confidence and trust as in the earnest endeavor to build her a home of her own. Any woman who has tact, forethought, and patience with her husband need not despair of owning eventually just such a home as The Hamilton.

13

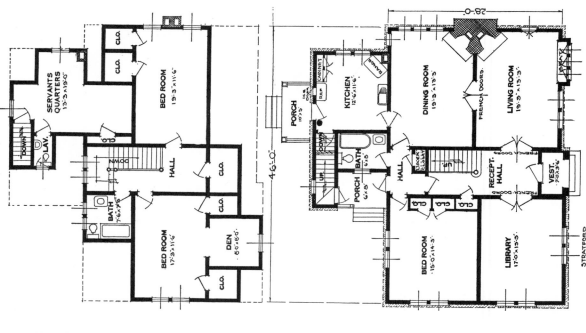

The STRATFORD   (Size 46x28')

If those who occupy homes like The Stratford are not happy it is because they have violated some natural law, or are not conscious of the fact that happiness is a condition of the mind and comes as the result of the mastery of one's moods. It is not a thing to be purchased at a price, but rather a fact to be recognized or accepted, regardless.

14

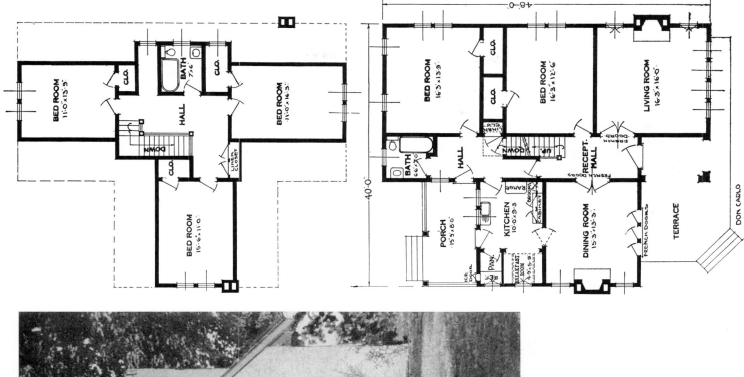

Our six-room plan for this design can be built at lower cost.

The DON CARLO   (Size 40x48')

There is something in the nature of a woman that calls for seclusion in the home life. Presumably it is the maternal instinct that instinctively leads to privacy for protection. The woman whose inner self calls for a freer life in a private home, will obey the most sacred impulse if she patiently persists until such call is answered by the possession of The Don Carlo.

15

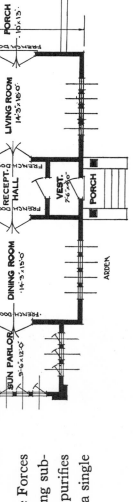

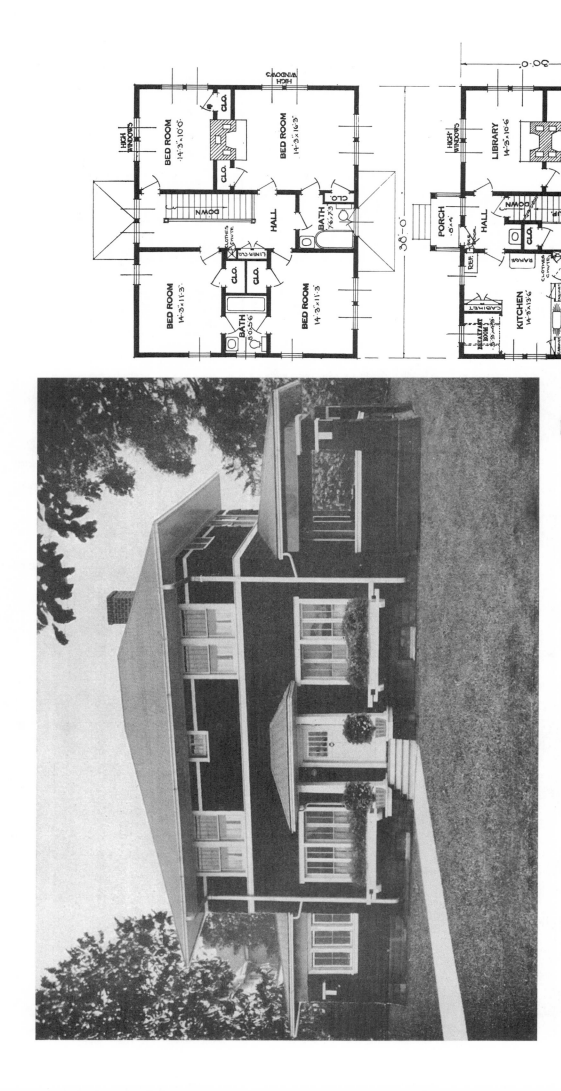

The ARDEN (Size 38x30')

Peace, power and plenty come to those who form an affinity with the Forces that work for the continuous advancement of humanity. The underlying substance which promotes all human progress is love, and love is that which purifies and perfects. It is in the home of freedom, where two hearts have but a single thought that power is generated for prosperity.

16

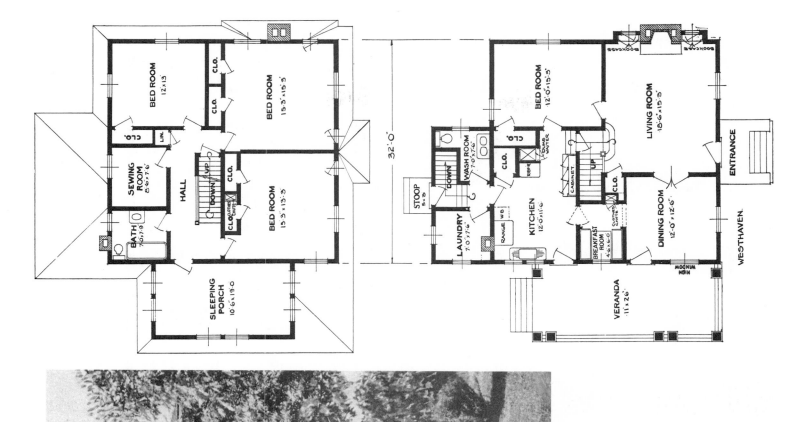

The WESTHAVEN (Size 32x32')

Spacious homey homes like the Westhaven are usually constructed in the suburbs by those whose generous natures lead them away from the cramped and crowded districts where limited space and unlimited noises tend to choke their creative thoughts during hours of meditation. Furthermore, The Westhaven is strictly practical as well as peaceful and restful, and its dignity is undeniable in any community.

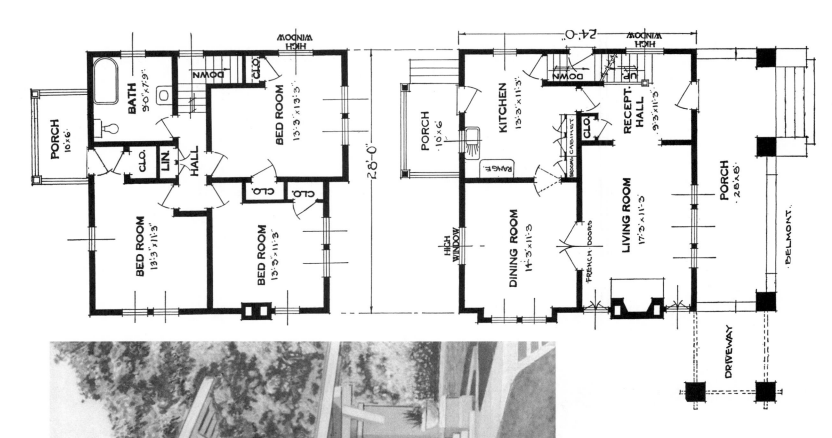

The BELMONT (Size 28x24')

Man's strength can easily be gauged by his faith in the strength of woman. Woman's intuition has always equalled, and in many instances surpassed, man's reason. Strong men know this vital principle of life and strive daily to keep harmonious the home in which dwells the heart and source of their strength. This is an easy task in beautiful new homes like The Belmont.

18

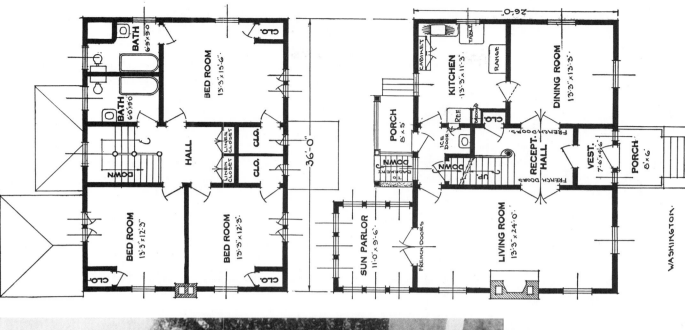

The WASHINGTON (Size 36x26')

When one looks thoughtfully at the colonial style of architecture as shown in The Washington, his thoughts go back to the days when the love of home and family were the most sacred emotions in the hearts of men. There are yet many with a steadfastness of purpose who inwardly long for the colonial days, and to such The Washington will be an inspiration.

19

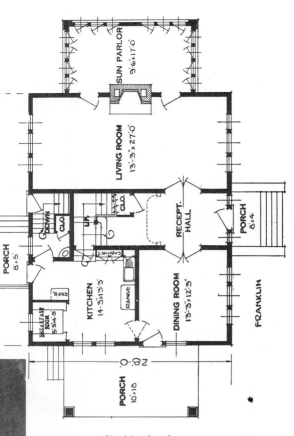

Neither time nor conditions can change the dignity and beauty of this style of colonial architecture.

The FRANKLIN (Size 36x28')

Nothing beautiful or sweet grows in the darkness. Light and sunshine are the superior forces that develop the finest and purest qualities in all nature. No work of the Creator is so sensitive to environment as woman, nor so susceptible to culture in the light and sunshine of appreciation and kindness such as may be expressed in homes like The Franklin.

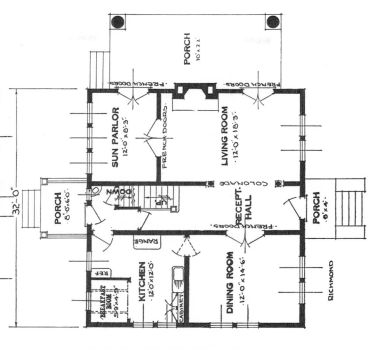

The RICHMOND   (Size 32x28')

There can be no freedom nor peace of mind in mature life for those who do not pay the price in youth. The price of freedom and peace is independence gained through sacrifice. Those who make the sacrifices necessary to enable them to own The Richmond will turn the present seeming desert into the paradise of their early dreams.

The WESTMORELAND (Size 36x36')

The life that would be complete, that would be sweet and sane as well as strong must be softened and enriched by a love of nature and all things beautiful. In no other way has man proven his onward and upward march as in the creation of beautiful homes like The Westmoreland. Such homes are civilization's guide-posts on the path of progress.

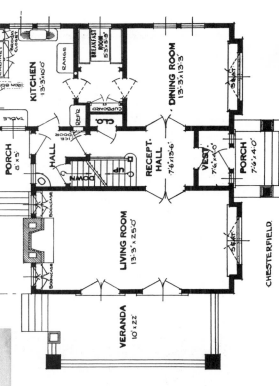

Character of sterling worth is invariably developed in the home.

The CHESTERFIELD (Size 36x26')

Out of homes of The Chesterfield class come men of victorious bearing whose voices, manners and expressions inspire confidence and trust. Such homes are, as a rule, owned by men of quick decision, keen perceptive faculties and indomitable wills. Truly the comforts of such homes as The Chesterfield should not pass with a single generation.

23

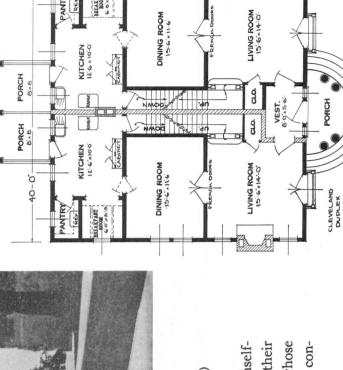

Second floor plan labels:
BED ROOM 12'-0"x13'-3" · CLO. · BED ROOM 12'-0"x11'-6" · CLO. · BED ROOM 15'-0"x11'-3" · CLO. · LINEN · BATH 6'-6"x9'-6" · HALL · ATTIC · UP · DOWN · VEST. 8'-0"x5'-6" · BALCONY

First floor plan labels:
PANTRY · REF. · BREAKFAST ROOM 6'-6"x5'-3" · KITCHEN 12'-6"x10'-0" · CABINET · RANGE · DINING ROOM 15'-6"x11'-6" · FRENCH DOORS · LIVING ROOM 15'-6"x14'-0" · PORCH 6'x8 · VEST. 8'-0"x5'-6" · CLO. · DOWN · UP · PORCH · CLEVELAND DUPLEX · 38'-0" · 40'-0"

If interested ask for our one-family plan for this design.

The CLEVELAND DUPLEX   (Size 40x38')

All the creative, uplifting forces of nature conspire to help those who unselfishly seek a home of comfort and refinement where the finer qualities of their
natures may be cultivated and their field of endeavor broadened.   Those whose
honest efforts enable them to build The Cleveland Duplex for a home may con-
fidently expect the peace of mind to which they are justly entitled.

24

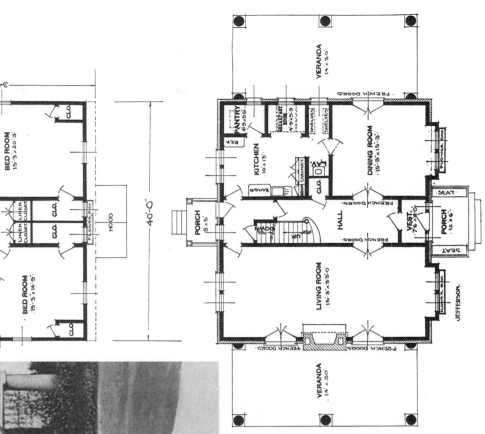

The JEFFERSON (Size 40x34')

The faculty of inhabitiveness (the love of one's place of birth) is developed far more in the young man or woman whose home has been one of sunshine and freedom than in those whose place of habitation has been sordid and cramped. One would naturally expect the youth from The Jefferson to reflect all of the joy and purity of a wholesome environment.

25

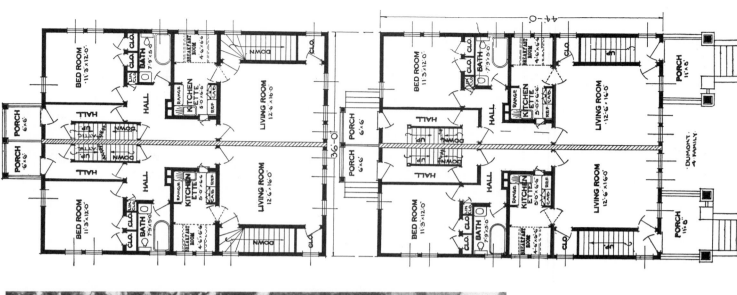

The DUMONT—Four-Family   (Size 36x44')

Study the floor plans of the Dumont four-family carefully, for it required weeks of thought and years of experience to install in such a given space all of the comforts and conveniences necessary for four separate families. Not a foot of space is wasted, not an inch missed in the location of every window and door, and not a single point overlooked that means comfort for the modern, efficient housewife.

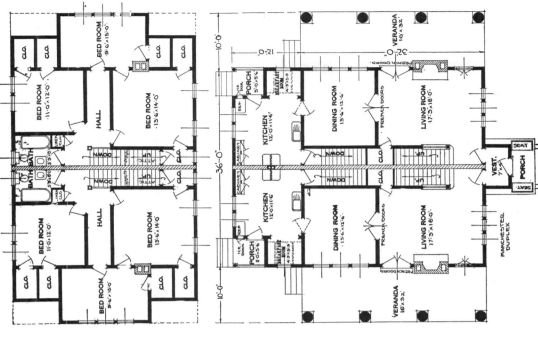

If interested ask for our one-family plan for this design.

The MANCHESTER—Duplex (Size 36x32')

The Manchester is a masterpiece in architecture, whether constructed as a single home or as a duplex. Its stately individuality causes it to stand alone in any community as a mansion of rare grace and permanent beauty; and yet so carefully have its designers considered economy in construction, that it is well within the means of those contemplating the erection of a two-family design.

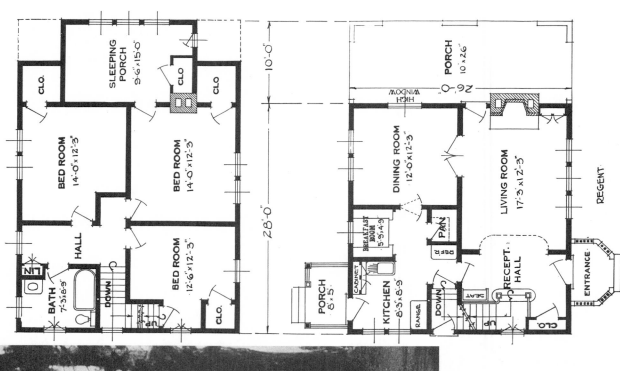

The REGENT (Size 28x26')

The Regent was designed for those who wish a home of distinction, decidedly different from the many well-known types. There is carefully combined in this home, grace, character, and comfort, and so cleverly have these three features been blended, it will stand as a thing of beauty in any community, regardless of neighboring mansions.

28

BED ROOM 11'-3"x10'-0"

CLO.

CLO.

BED ROOM 11'-3"x14'-0"

HALL

LIN.

LIN.

BATH 7'x9'

CLO.

DOWN

BED ROOM 11'-3"x14'-0"

STORAGE

CLO.

24'-0"

BOOKCASE

BOOKCASE

HIGH WINDOW

DINING ROOM 11'-3"x12'-6"

RANGE

LIVING ROOM 23'-0"x13'-6"

PORCH 8x5

ICE DOOR

REFR

KITCHEN 9x9

CABINET

BREAKFAST ROOM 4'-9"x5'-9"

DOWN

DOWN

SOMERSET

PORCH 10'x12'

The SOMERSET (Size 24x28')

Homes founded on mutual interest are practically proof against the divorce evil. This is true because like attracts like, and when two individuals direct their hearts and efforts toward one single purpose, such, for instance, as the building and making happy a home of The Somerset design, they daily learn to know each other better because they think each other's thoughts.

29

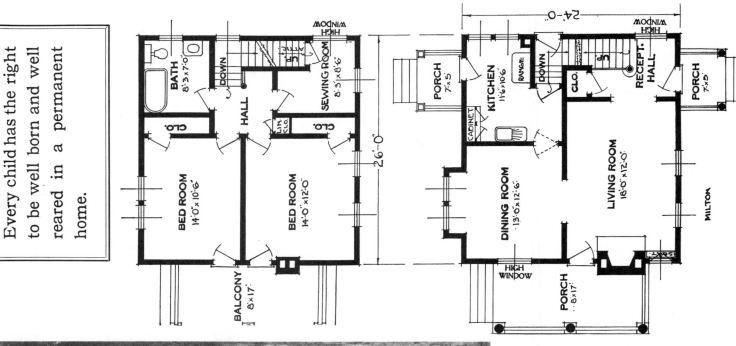

Every child has the right to be well born and well reared in a permanent home.

Second Floor Plan

BATH 8'3"x7'0"

DOWN

SEWING ROOM 8'3"x8'6"

HALL

LIN. CLO.

CLO.

CLO.

BED ROOM 14'0"x10'6"

BED ROOM 14'0"x12'0"

HIGH WINDOW

26'-0"

BALCONY 8x17'

First Floor Plan

24'-0"

PORCH 7x5'

KITCHEN 11'6"x10'6"

RANGE

DOWN

CLO.

RECEPT. HALL

PORCH 7x5'

HIGH WINDOW

CABINET

DINING ROOM 13'6"x12'6"

LIVING ROOM 18'0"x12'0"

MILTON

HIGH WINDOW

PORCH 8x17'

The MILTON (Size 26x24')

As the human mind unfolds, new possibilities are seen and new strength is developed for greater tasks. Those who see in The Milton a home of exceptional advantages, comforts and conveniences, and firmly fix their hearts on its possession, can surely develop the strength necessary to enable them to materialize the mental pictures which they hold.

30

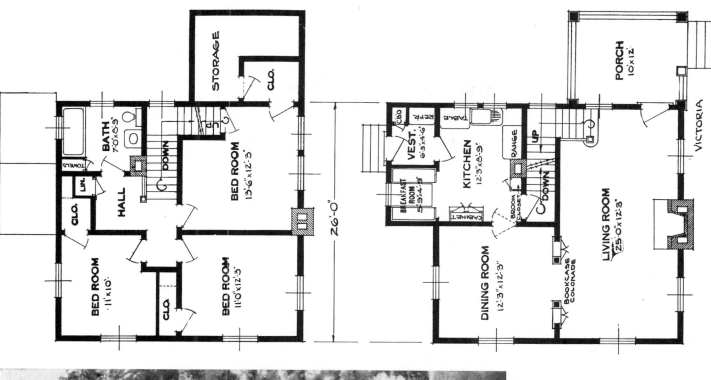

The VICTORIA (Size 26x26')

A child seldom becomes a burden on society whose home life has been one of happiness and contentment. The home is the localized center from which initial impulses for good or evil go out. Those who select The Victoria as a home in which to purify the environment for their children may well pay the debt to humanity which all of us owe.

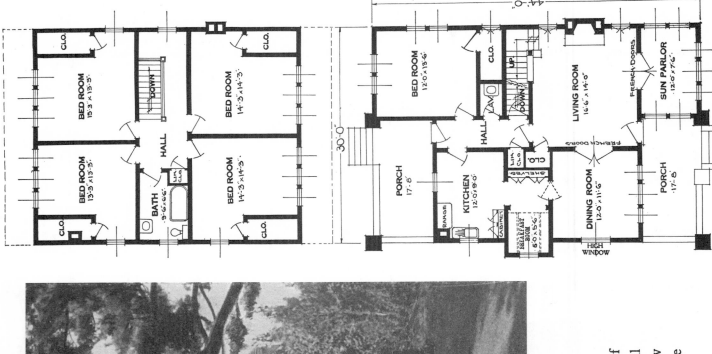

Floor plan labels (second floor, left): CLO. BED ROOM 15'-3"x13'-3" | BED ROOM 14'-3"x14'-3" CLO. | DOWN | HALL | CLO. BED ROOM 13'-3"x13'-3" | BATH 9'-6"x6'-6" LIN. CLO. | BED ROOM 14'-3"x14'-3" CLO.

Floor plan labels (first floor, right): 44'-0" | 30'-0" | BED ROOM 12'-0"x13'-6" | CLO. | UP | LIVING ROOM 16'-6"x14'-0" | FRENCH DOORS | SUN PARLOR 12'-0"x7'-6" | PORCH 17'-6" | HALL | LAV. | DOWN | LIN. CLO. | CLO. SHELVED | FRENCH DOORS | DINING ROOM 12'-0"x11'-6" | PORCH 17'-6" | KITCHEN 12'-0"x9'-0" | RANGE | CABINET | BREAKFAST ROOM 6'-0"x5'-6" | HIGH WINDOW | KENDALL

The KENDALL (Size 30x44')

Sunshine is to the physical body what joy is to the heart. Those frail of body should seek the sun porches of homes of The Kendall plan, and those frail of heart can find inimitable balm in the building and making complete a new home and a new environment. Health and home joy come to those who prepare expectantly for their reception.

32

The GLENDALE (Size 28x34')

The human mind is a most powerful magnet, and never fails to attract to us those things and conditions on which our hearts are earnestly and constantly centered. The Glendale is within reach of him who wills and fears not the petty thorns of sacrifice, knowing that these will be forgotten or remembered with delight when the goal is finally realized.

33

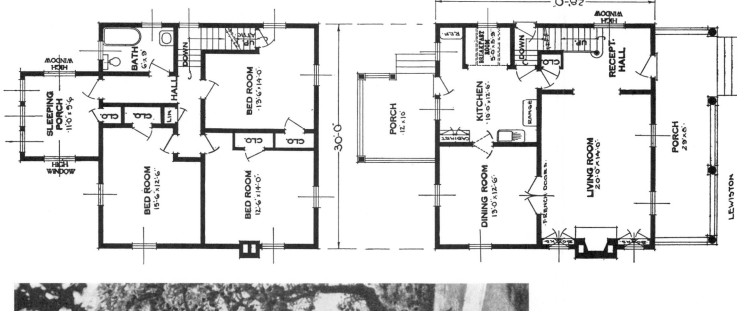

The LEWISTON (Size 30x28')

Life is a glory instead of a grind to those who are monthly placing their earnings on a new home of their own, and their spare time in beautifying the lawn and garden. There is a peace which comes with the possession of homes like The Lewiston which cannot be gained, even in a house of granite owned by a landlord.

34

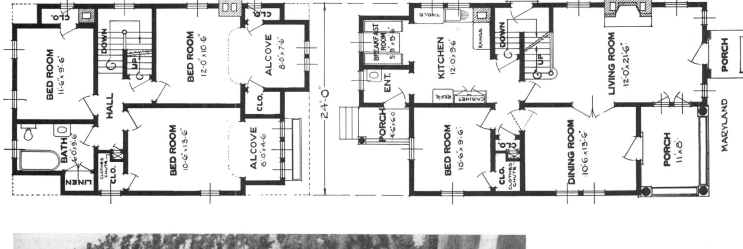

The MARYLAND (Size 24x36')

Homes are not constructed alone of brick and stone and wood. These are merely the materials out of which the walls are fashioned. Artistic structures like The Maryland are simply inviting, comfortable places where ambitious hearts can quietly and undisturbed build homes of culture, refinement and love which neither climate nor man can mar.

35

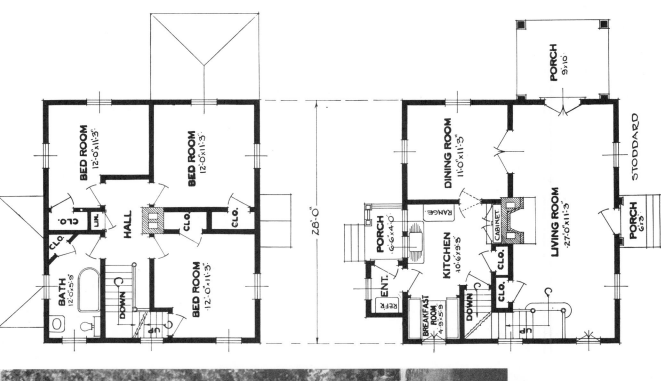

The STODDARD (Size 28x24')

The reward for a thing well done is to have done it. Homes built by others can never give us the inner satisfaction which comes as the reward for hours and weeks spent in the careful planning of a home of our own. In erecting The Stoddard in accordance with their ideals, many will learn with peculiar delight the care-joy of home building.

36

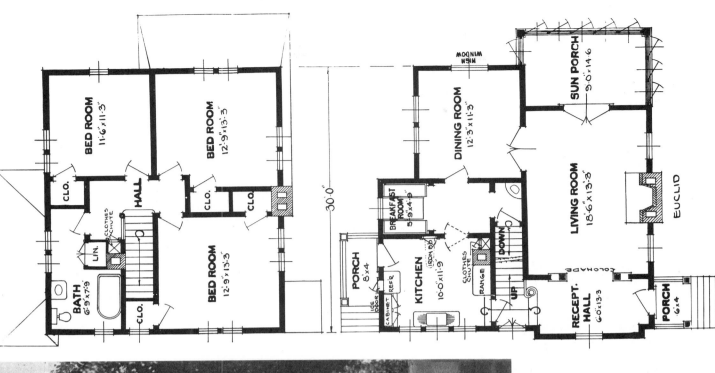

BED ROOM 11'6"×11'3"

BED ROOM 12'9"×13'3"

CLO.

HALL

CLO.

CLO.

BATH 6'9"×7'9"

LIN.

CLOTHES CHUTE

CLO.

BED ROOM 12'9"×13'3"

30'0"

DINING ROOM 12'3"×11'3"

SUN PORCH 9'0"×14'6"

HIGH WINDOW

BREAKFAST ROOM 5'9"×4'9"

PORCH 8'×4

KITCHEN 10'0"×11'9"

ICE BOX

CABINET

REFR.

CLOTHES CHUTE

RANGE

DOWN

UP

LIVING ROOM 18'6"×13'3"

COLONNADE

RECEPT. HALL 6'0"×13'3"

PORCH 6'4

EUCLID

The EUCLID (Size 30x30')

The education that counts in life's competition is the education that elevates and ennobles. The race for supremacy in the sensible pursuit of sane business is not won by the fleet-footed but by the strong. In private homes like The Euclid there is a chance for children to absorb the essentials of a sound, unselfish education.

37

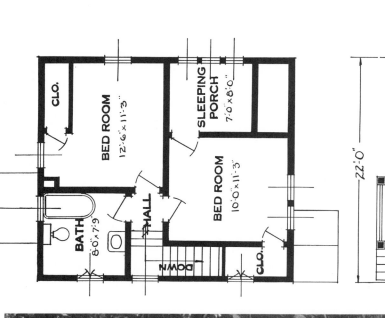

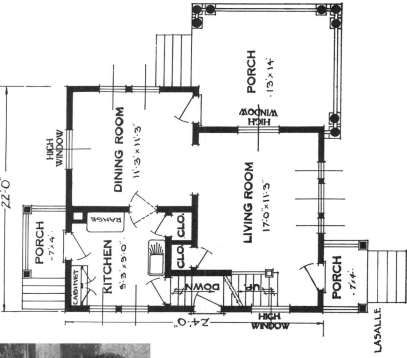

LASALLE

The LA SALLE (Size 22x24')

Could all bachelors purchase insurance against mishaps and discords in marriage and be assured that their life companions would be real helpmates in the building and keeping of their homes, contracts for houses similar to The La Salle would be let by the thousands, and the loss of help from the workshops and offices would paralyze business for the time.

38

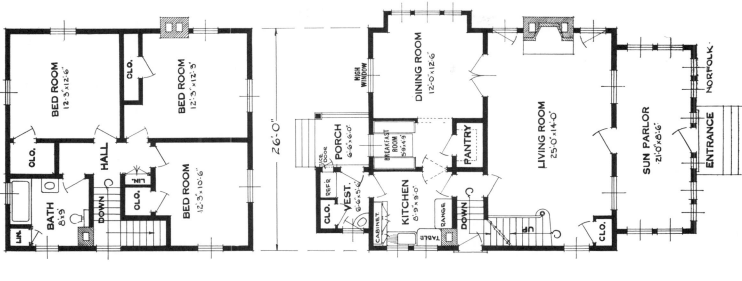

The NORFOLK (Size 26x28')

Men and women never so fully realize their oneness with life and the natural Law of Perpetual Progress as when their best efforts are directed toward the creation of a home and family. To build The Norfolk for a home, and to make that home vibrate with joy and mutual interest, is to join the front ranks for permanent advancement.

39

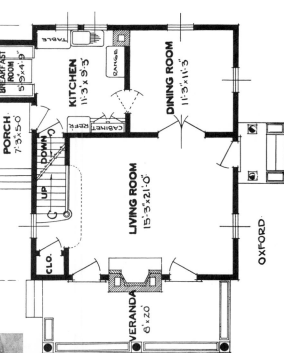

The OXFORD (Size 28x22')

When freedom and joy are the wife's share in homes like The Oxford they become the child's heritage, and a happy childhood is an imperative preparation for a happy maturity. The sacred memories of a joyful home have kept many a man from losing his balance and self-respect. We would have little need for prisons if all children could enjoy the early home life to which they are entitled.

40

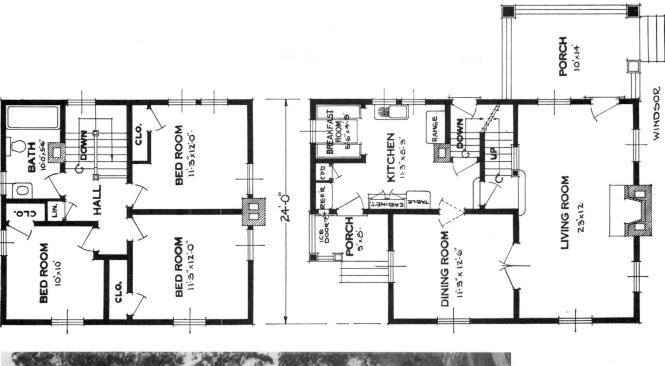

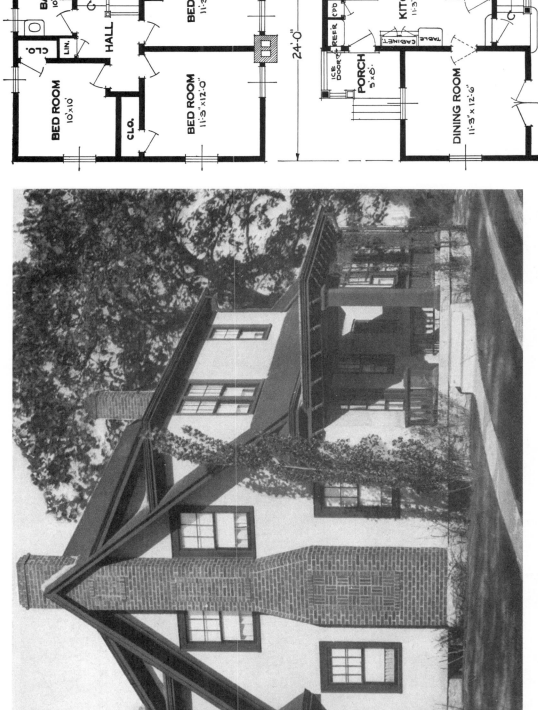

The WINDSOR (Size 24x26')

Selfishness seldom strangles the man whose pride and ambition lead him to build a home of The Windsor design. Pride in one's home is the fire that kindles power for success, and ambition is the invisible voice that ever calls man successward. It is home and its accompanying sentiments that develop character of sterling quality.

41

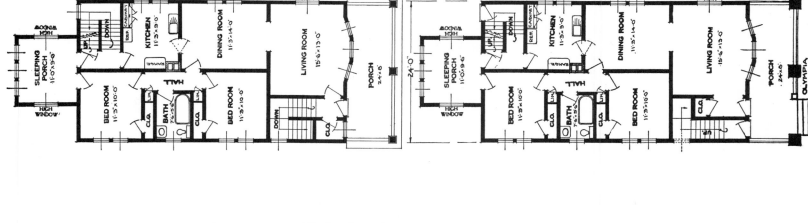

The OLYMPIA (Size 24x44')

The home that nearest approaches in comforts and conveniences the private residence is the modern two-family, such as The Olympia. While the occupants of such dwellings are denied certain private privileges to be found in the individual home, yet there are many practical and desirable features for those who figure them out from a monetary standpoint.

42

The BRUNSWICK (Size 28x48')

Two-family houses are most desirable for adults who seek the constant companionship of companionable people; and for such The Brunswick stands for all that could be sought in staunch construction and practical comforts. It is a departure from the usual two-family type, and many will appreciate the home-like appearance added by the separate entrances.

43

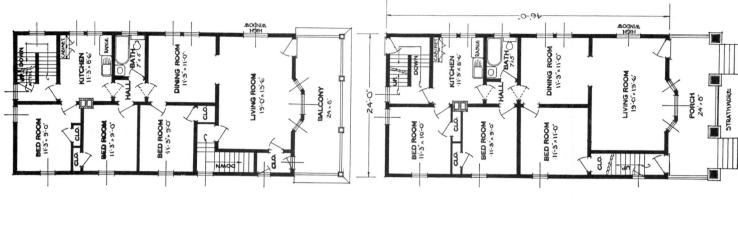

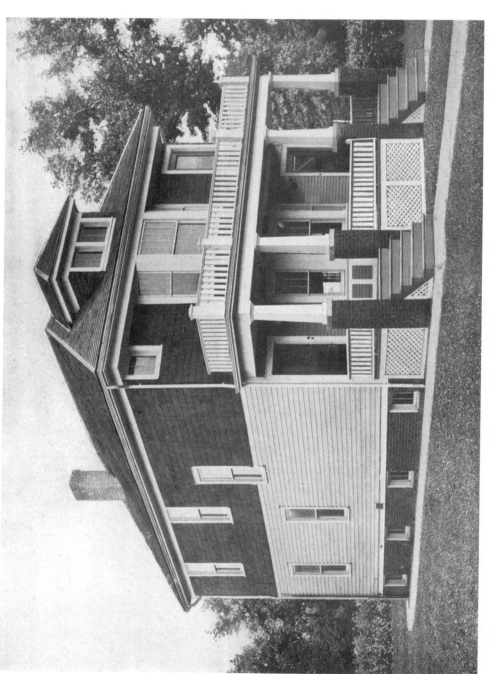

The STRATHMORE (Size 24x46')

For those who build homes, either for sale or for rent, the two-family of The Strathmore style will prove to be a most profitable investment. Few investments pay larger or more regular dividends, and the security is easily converted into cash if conditions demand. Economy in construction is the most notable feature of this practical design.

44

The BELVEDERE (Size 26x52')

The Belvedere is beautiful, practical and decidedly correct in every detail, and as a two-family it is offered as one of the most distinctive to be found. The designers had a reason for every touch to the exterior and a cause for every comfort afforded in the floor plan. A knowledge of present-day demands, coupled with exactness of detail, developed the Belvedere.

45

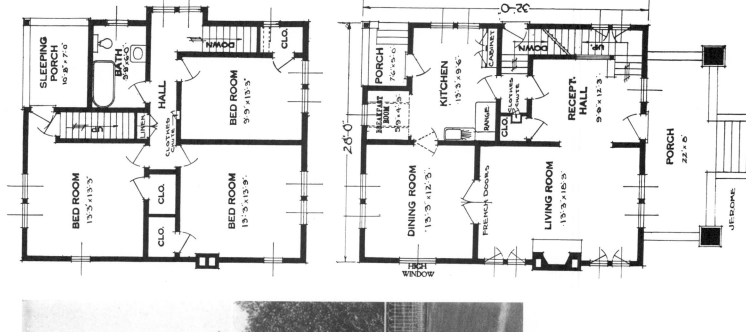

The JEROME (Size 28x32')

The unprecedented progress of the American people can be attributed more than anything else to the freedom which American women enjoy in the home. When a woman of culture selects a home like The Jerome for her kingdom in which to practice the principles of freedom and co-operation, a new star is manifest in the firmament of civilization.

46

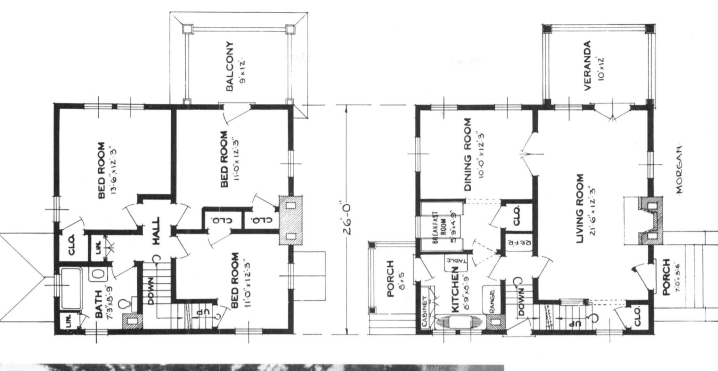

The MORGAN (Size 26x26')

All obstacles stand aside for him who firmly fixes his gaze on a coveted goal, and goes forward with a steady step and a strong heart. Homes in The Morgan class are within reach of those whose esthetic natures and ideals demand beauty in abundance, and whose wills calmly and fearlessly affirm that substitutes are unacceptable.

47

The LINCOLN (Size 24x34')

The strength and union of America has been developed and kept sacred by liberty and home-loving people. Freedom and democracy as enjoyed and expressed in the home are the principles which promote our progress as a nation. Could every family enjoy in a home like The Lincoln the freedom to which all are justly entitled, strife would cease and crime would be unknown.

48

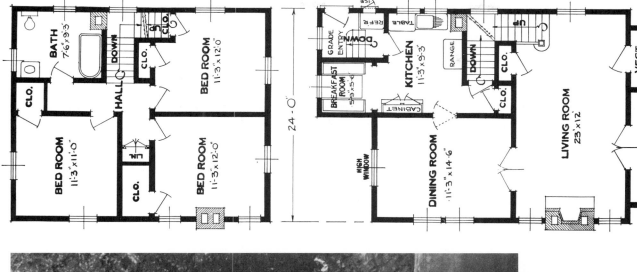

The BRISTOL (Size 24x28')

To the wife and children home means infinitely more than to the husband whose duties are elsewhere. To him it is a place for recreation and rest, but to them it is their kingdom. The hearts of many wives will go out to The Bristol, not with selfish designs, but with earnest maternal longings for better conditions for the culture and refinement of their children.

49

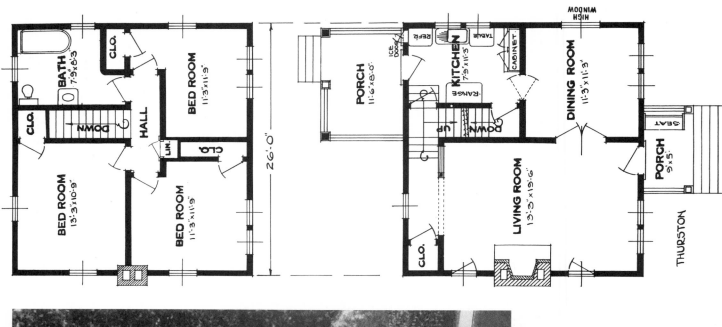

The THURSTON   (Size 26x24')

When one wishes to build a home, there are three points to be considered: first, the size of his pocketbook; second, his family and their requirements; and third, the type of house out of which he can realize the greatest profits if it becomes necessary to dispose of it. The Thurston is not only a practical house for a home, but is always the salable type.

50

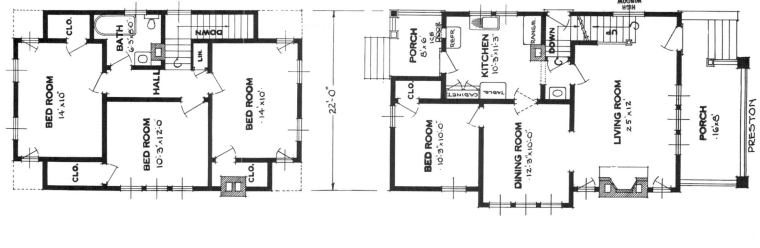

The PRESTON (Size 22x34')

The hearth that glows with good fellowship warms chilly hearts and drives out the dampness of discord and disappointments. Such hearths are guarded constantly by women who worship sacred home ideals, and who turn a deaf ear to the voice of gossip. The Preston will make an ideal home for those who yearn for better conditions in which to demonstrate the power of right thought.

51

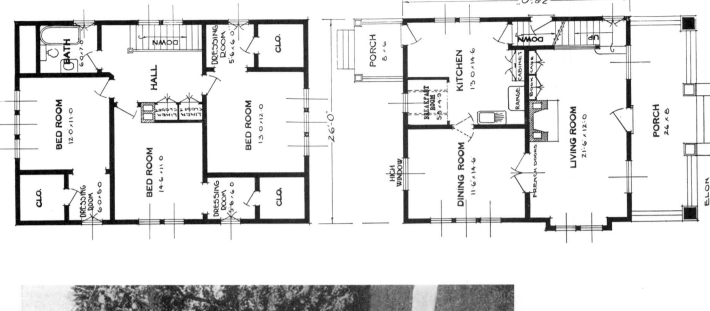

The ELON (Size 26x28')

The club rooms are not filled by men whose earnings have gone to purchase or build homes of The Elon character, for where a man's treasure is there will his heart be also. Man loves best those things which have cost most in earnest effort and self-denial, and there is little outside attraction for him whose longing for a home is satisfied.

52

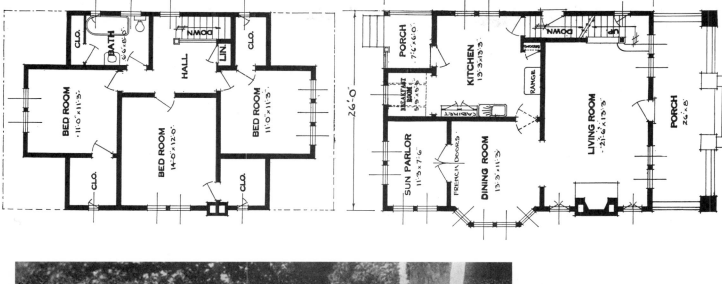

The EDENTON (Size 26x34')

The first step in the path of progress is to fix in the mind a clear vision of better conditions, better surroundings and a better place for normal and unhampered growth. Growth comes from freedom of thought and an inner feeling of independence. In no other place can a family so well realize this desired freedom as in a home of their own—such, perhaps, as The Edenton.

53

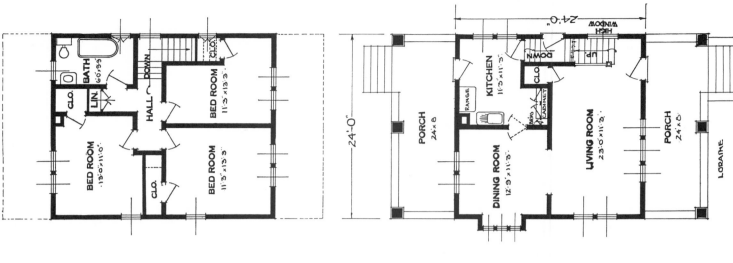

The LORAINE (Size 24x24')

Happiness is the friend of harmony, of truth, of beauty, of simplicity, and does not abide with low ideals, with selfishness, idleness and discord. It is most frequently found in beautiful, new homes like The Loraine which have been built by those whose ability to appreciate the beautiful, the good, the true, has been kept alive by the development of their best and noblest thoughts.

54

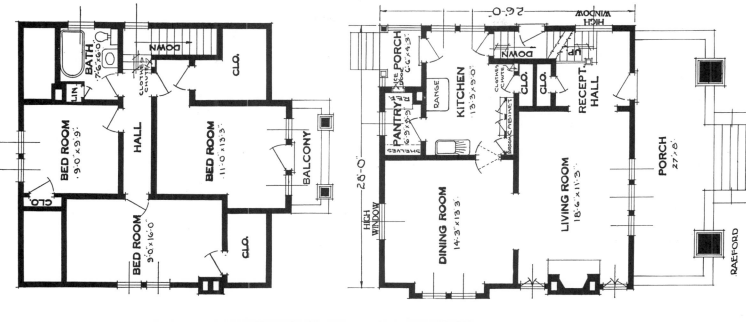

The RAEFORD (Size 28x26')

It is never the size nor monetary value of a home that grips and holds the heart of a child as the years lead him into manhood. Instead it is the sympathy, companionship and love demonstrated by contented parents who have early learned that life is fuller and more abundant in a convenient home of their own, such as The Raeford.

55

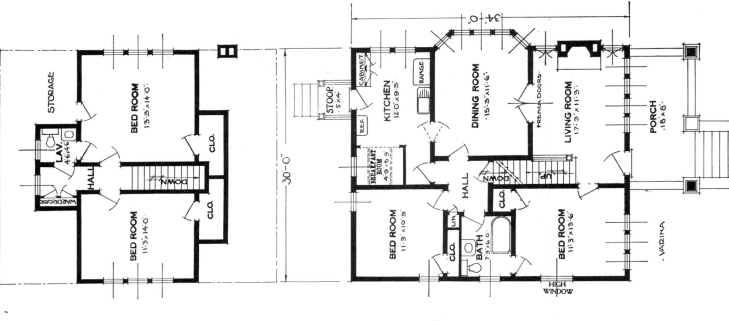

The VARINA (Size 30x34')

There is something void in the being of a man who has the care neither of a home nor a family. Within the walls of his selfish fancy he may boast of his freedom and life of ease, but he is a prisoner indeed who knows not the joys of conjugal companionship, and the care and responsibility of a home, perhaps in the class of The Varina.

56

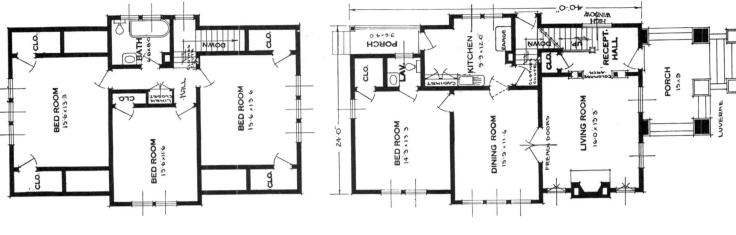

The LUVERNE (Size 24x40')

Every child has the right to be born and reared in an environment free from discord and paternal unrest. It is far easier for parents to maintain a wholesome atmosphere for their children in a private home like The Luverne than it is in a crowded tenement or apartment house where conditions are neither sanitary nor homelike.

57

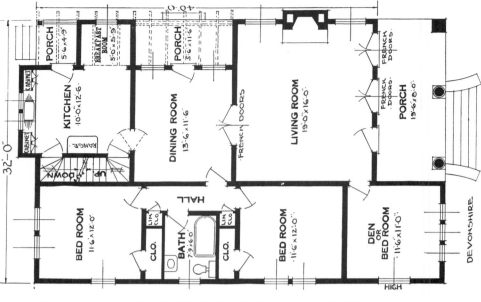

The DEVONSHIRE (Size 32x48')

The happiest homes, like the happiest marriages, are those in which the woman takes the most sacred part, and uses her secret power to guide for permanent good. Any woman who is mated to the man of her choice, and is permitted to enjoy her freedom in a home like The Devonshire, can surely make it a paradise for worldly peace.

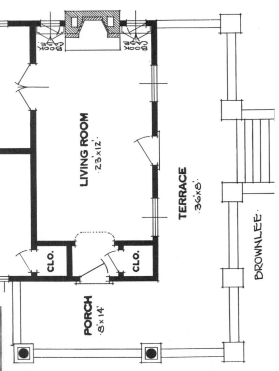

Floor plan labels: 28'-0", REF'R, TABLE, KITCHEN, RANGE, CABINET, GAS, NON. 10.9'-6"x9'-0", BREAKFAST ROOM 4'-9"x5'-9", DOWN, UP, HALL, DINING ROOM 13'-3"x11'-0", DOOR CASE, DOOR CASE, BED ROOM 13'-3"x11'-0", CLO., BATH 9'-3"x7'-9", LIN., BED ROOM 13'-3"x11'-0", LIVING ROOM 23'x12', CLO., CLO., TERRACE 36'x8', PORCH 8'x14', BROWNLEE

The BROWNLEE   (Size 28x44')

To know the value of right environment is one of the first steps in the mastery of self. It is impossible for anyone to think his best thoughts or do his best work when his home life is not in keeping with his ideals. Those who firmly fix their hearts on The Brownlee for a home may be assured of the refining influence which its possession will bring.

59

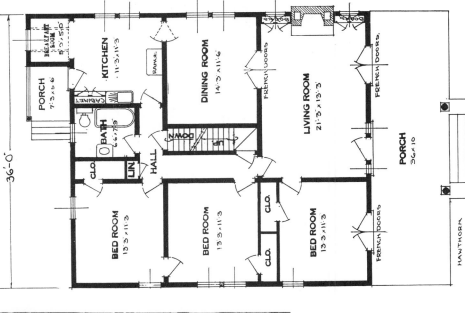

A good home is a debt which every man owes to his wife and family. He will always be in debt while he lives in a rented house.

The HAWTHORN   (Size 36x38')

A man is often judged as much by the home he builds as by the company he keeps or the clothes he wears. One would expect to find the owner of The Hawthorn a man of good judgment and thoughtful purpose, of influence and solid character. Men who select and build homes of this style are as a rule sentinels of progress in their communities.

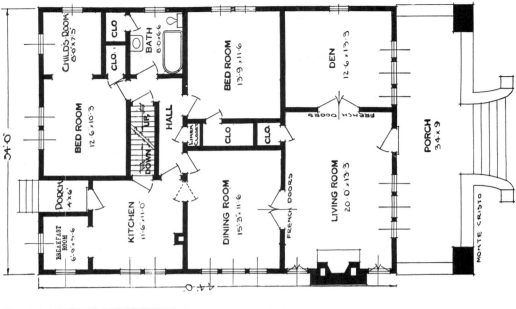

The MONTE CRISTO (Size 34x44')

Those who plan a home for a place of rest and contentment and in the planning think not of children and their comforts and joys, know little of the law of love and the underlying principles of happiness and mental growth. In The Monte Cristo the child's room is most thoughtfully arranged, and happy will be the occupants of this home if they are blessed with the care of children.

61

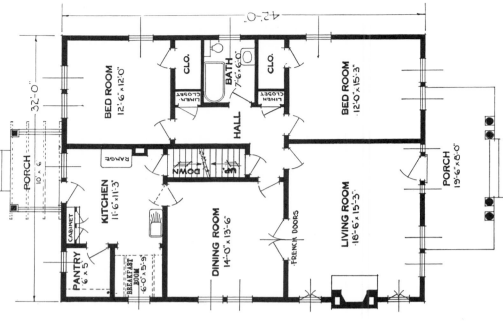

The "guess and cut" way of constructing homes is fast giving way to more modern methods.

The CORNELL (Size 32x42')

True peace and enduring happiness are found only by those who unselfishly seek to develop the best in themselves and in others. The most natural place for such growth and influence is in the individual home where inner strength is constantly developed by conscious freedom, and fear is shut out and destroyed by a sacred purpose.

No type of dwelling has ever increased in popularity so rapidly as the California bungalow. It has become a model for all the world.

The CARDENAS (Size 32x42')

The price of a good woman's complete love is appreciation, affection, sympathy and a home—a home of her own in which these virtues may be proudly and happily expressed. Happy will be the man who awakens to the importance of this vital fact and early makes the sacrifices necessary to realize his highest ambitions in a home like The Cardenas.

63

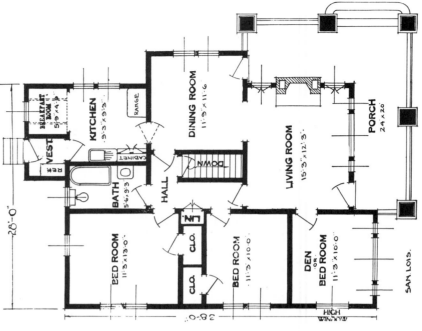

The SAN LOIS (Size 28x38')

It lies within the secret power of every intelligent woman to make the home happy which by her intuition she selects and helps to establish as an institution of culture and refinement. When a home of the decided character of the San Lois is erected at the bidding of a thoughtful woman, society's call for social example in the home life is answered.

64

The RADCLIFF (Size 28x44')

Some are seeking in an inexpensive home the massive coziness of a California bungalow of expensive proportions and for those The Radcliff was especially fashioned. The bigness of the columns and porch effect, the French doors and large living room give all of the welcome offered by many homes that would double its construction cost.

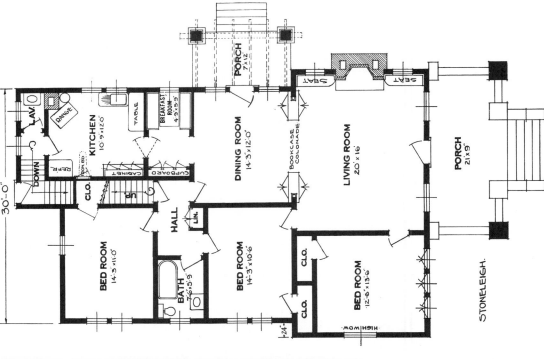

Men can produce far more when there is harmony and affection in the home.

STONELEIGH.

The STONELEIGH (Size 30x46′)

A child seldom becomes a burden on society whose home life has been one of happiness and contentment. The home is the localized center from which initial impulses for good or evil go out. Those who select The Stoneleigh as a home in which to purify the environment for their children may well pay the debt to humanity which all of us owe.

66

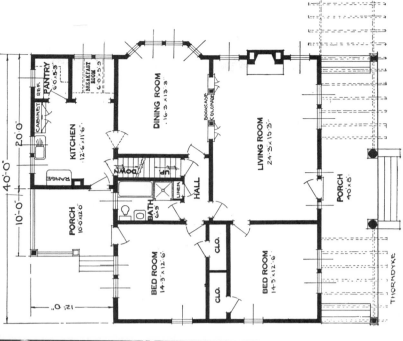

The woman who is fair to herself usually stays fair in the eyes of her husband.

The THORNDYKE (Size 40x42')

Unnecessary work is always unfair work. It is unfair for the housewife to be forced to take hundreds of unnecessary steps in the daily routine of housekeeping because she was not considered in the planning of the home. In arranging the floor plan for The Thorndyke, the architect considered first practical economy for the wife who does her own housework.

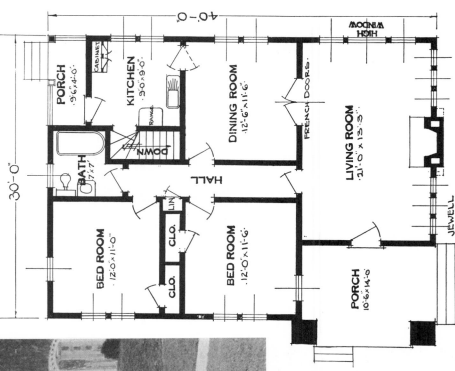

The JEWELL   (Size 30x40')

Everything in life either grows or decays, nothing remains the same. The man who is not planning and saving to build a home eventually, is allowing his will power to weaken and is going backward whether he is conscious of it or not. The homelike air of The Jewell will cause many to renew their energies and strive harder to realize their ambition for a home of their own.

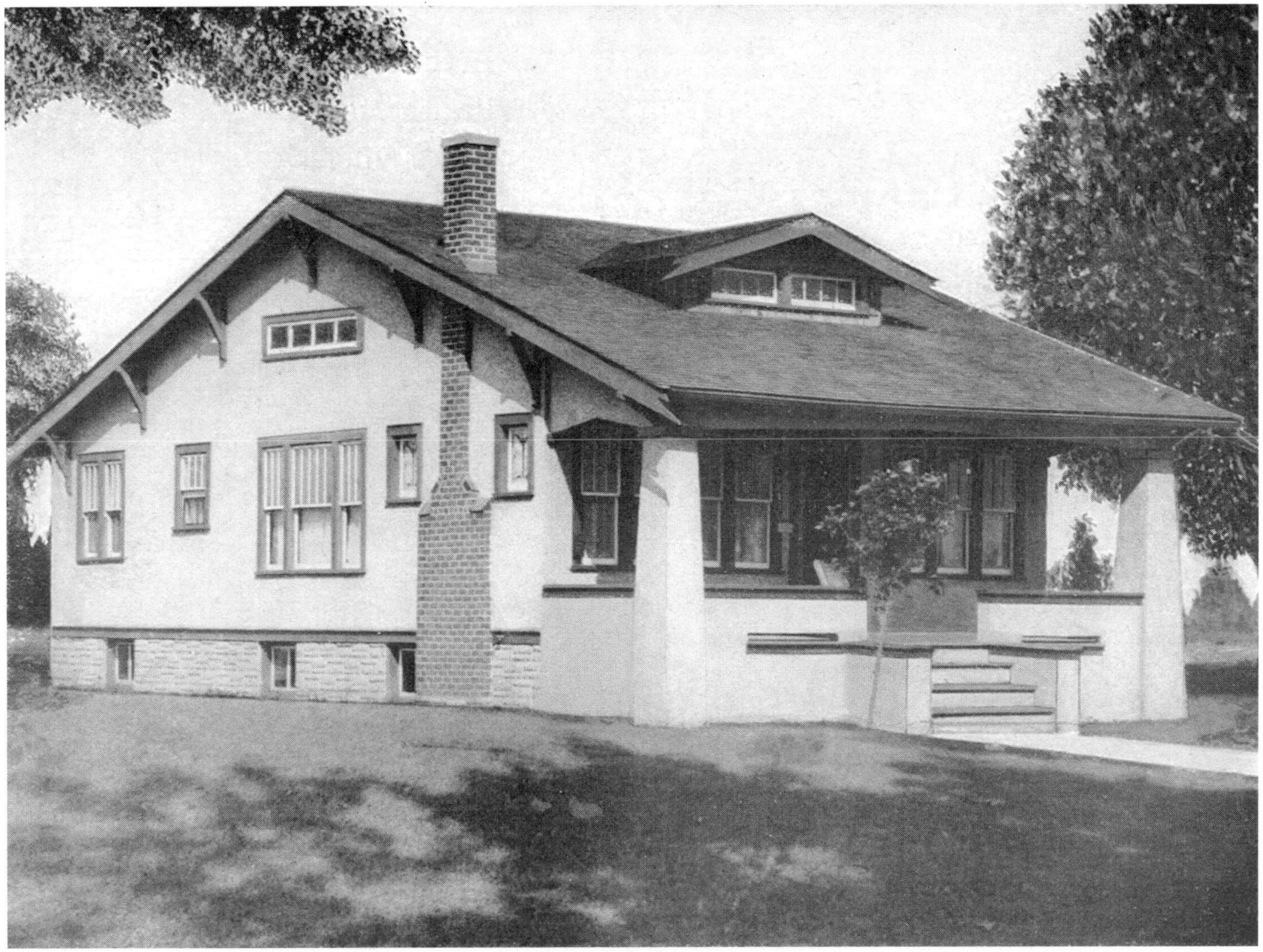

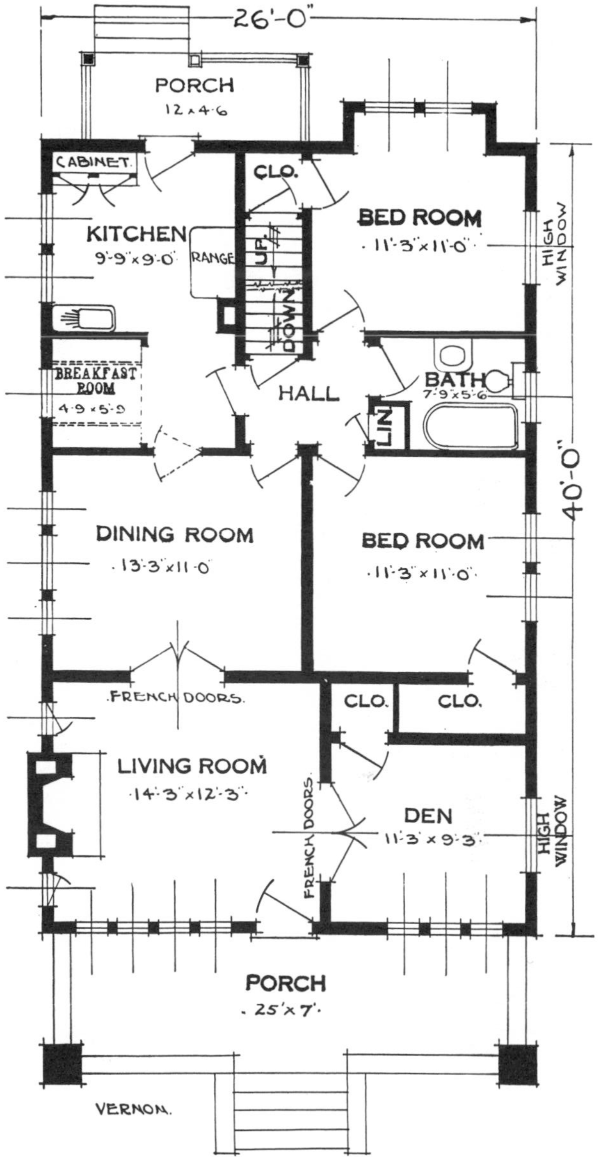
26'-0"
40'-0"
PORCH
12 x 4-6
CABINET
KITCHEN
9'-9" x 9'-0"
RANGE
BREAKFAST ROOM
4-9 x 5-9
CLO.
UP
DOWN
BED ROOM
11'-3" x 11'-0"
HIGH WINDOW
HALL
BATH
7-9 x 5-6
LIN
DINING ROOM
13'-3" x 11'-0"
BED ROOM
11'-3" x 11'-0"
FRENCH DOORS
CLO.
CLO.
LIVING ROOM
14'-3" x 12'-3"
FRENCH DOORS
DEN
11'-3" x 9'-3"
HIGH WINDOW
PORCH
25' x 7'
VERNON

The VERNON (Size 26x40')

Any woman can be easily measured by her love for home and children. Feminine beauty and sweetness of facial expression count as nothing when compared to these most sacred of human emotions. The gods smile on the man whose heart beats in unison with the lullabies of a happy mother as she cradles a living expression of love in a happy home like The Vernon.

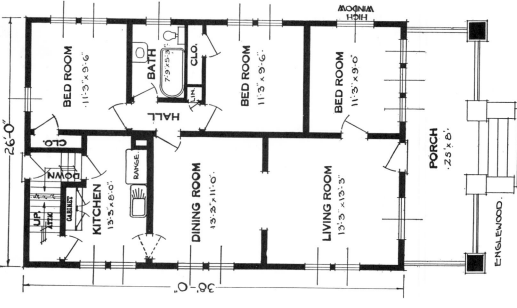

In the happiness of the home lies the health and strength of the whole family.

The ENGLEWOOD (Size 26x38')

Men change only as their environment and associates change. A good home and a good wife will enable any man to become stronger and more efficient. Any man is worthy of the highest trust who saves from his earnings sufficient to build The Englewood, and whose life companion is in sympathy with him and his work.

The colonial cottage, with a touch of the Western bungalow, fully meets the demand for a one-story, inexpensive home.

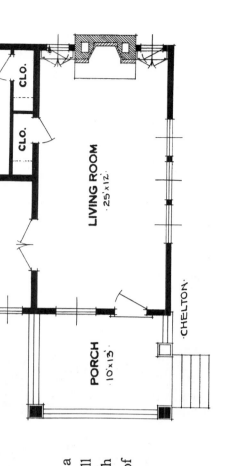

BED ROOM
11'×11'

BATH
7'0"×5'6"

CLO.

BED ROOM
12'-3"×11'-0"

26'-0"

DOWN

CABINET

IRON BD.

CLO.

BROOM CLOSET

CLOTHES CHUTE

HALL

CLO.

LIVING ROOM
25'×12'

KITCHEN
10'-0"×9'-3"

RANGE

LIN.

DINING ROOM
12'-3"×11'-0"

TABLE

REQ'D

BREAKFAST ROOM
4'-9"×5'-9"

PORCH
10'×13'

CHELTON

The CHELTON (Size 26x44')

The authority who said, "Give every family a home of their own with a garden and flowers and crime will vanish with a single generation,"—knew well the inspiration which everyone gains consciously or unconsciously from such surroundings. The Chelton style of architecture has ever been the theme of poets and the sons of song.

71

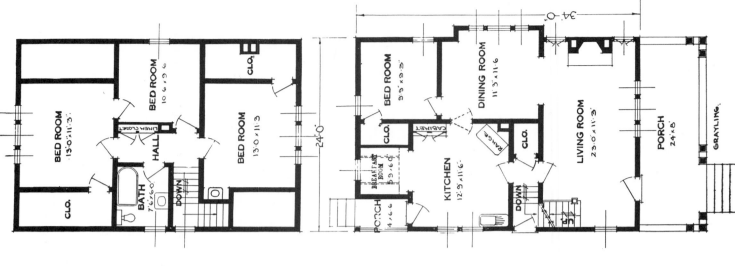

The GRAYLING (Size 24x34')

The care of a family means responsibility and responsibility in turn creates power. Just as it is more economical to own a home in the Grayling class than it is to pay rent, just so it is more economical for a man to support a family than to deny himself the breadth of vision which comes as the result of a happy union and a happy home life.

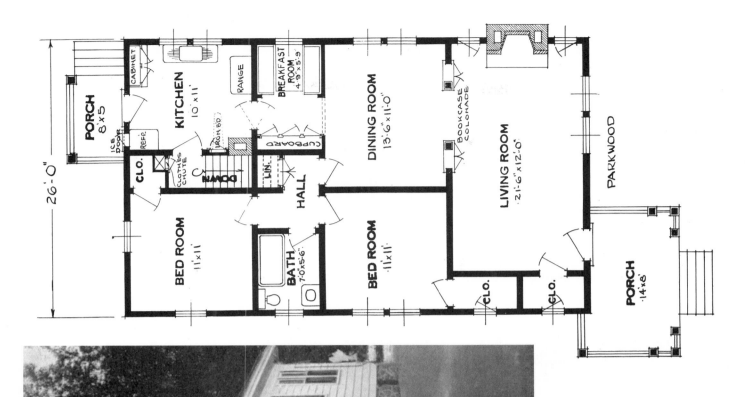

The PARKWOOD (Size 26x42')

It is a wonderful privilege to forget the unfortunate experiences and hideous images of yesterday and begin life anew in a home like The Parkwood. Happiness is for those who have the faculty to forget and live a new life daily "now and here," and nowhere is there such an opportunity for a full, new life as there is in a new home.

73

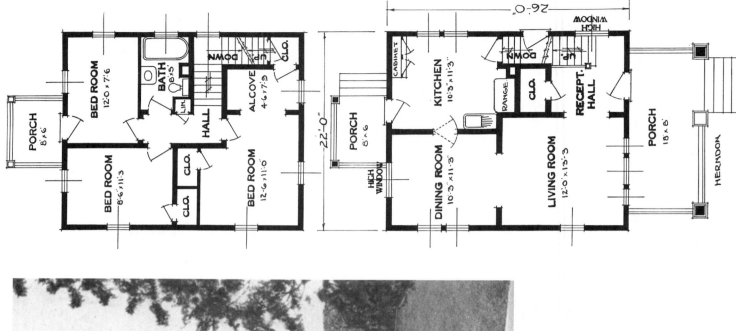

The HERNDON   (Size 22x26')

If all women knew how much easier it is for a man to be contented in a home he has helped to build and learned to love, countless numbers would lose no time in learning the cost and terms of payment on artistic homes of The Herndon type. Such homes are inexpensive to build, yet they hold a world of joy for earnest homeseekers.

74

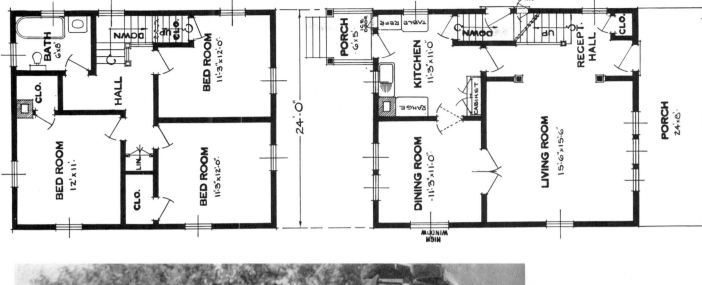

The KINGSTON (Size 24x28')

Summer, winter, rain or shine, your home's your home. It is a permanent structure, yet consider how many comforts its walls contain, and what a wonderful refuge it is when shelter is sought from the world of chilly indifference. No home can be more secure against unwholesome influences than The Kingston, if it be reinforced by staunch purpose and unselfish love.

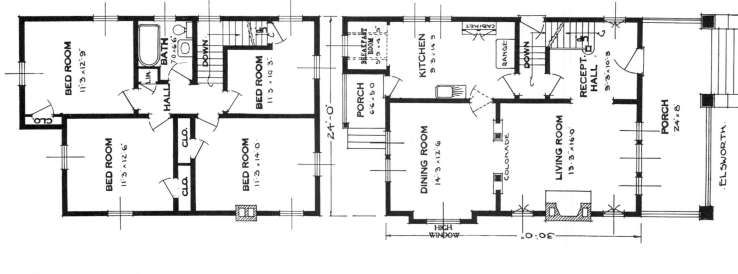

The ELSWORTH (Size 24x30')

Man loves those things which make him happy, which bring joy and sunshine into his life, and naturally he evades those things which cause him to become disheartened and discouraged. When one puts all of his earnings in a new home like The Elsworth and gives weeks of thought to every detail of arrangement, he finds a world of comfort and joy in its possession.

76

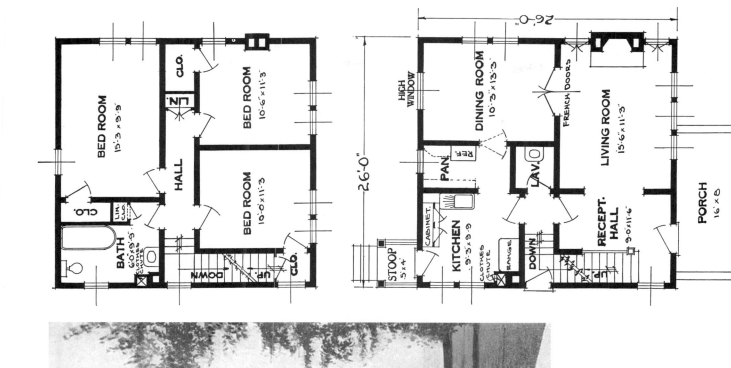

The BROOKLINE (Size 26x26')

Yearly scientists are learning more and more about the value of light in its relation to life, and yearly the city building departments are wisely watching the scientific discoveries in this connection, and are embodying in the building codes specific demands for more light in the homes. Like most other designs here shown, The Brookline will meet the view of the most exacting in this particular.

77

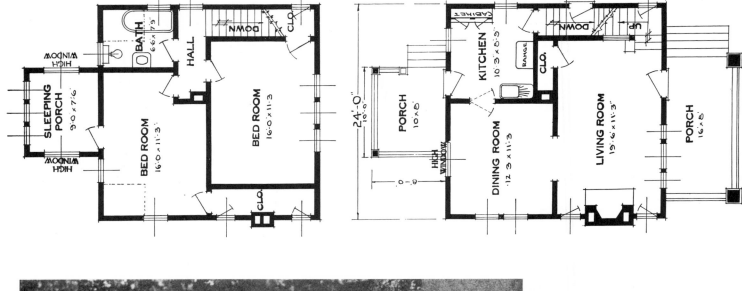

The GENESSEE (Size 24x24')

Those who put their savings into get-rich-quick schemes instead of homes of their own are, as a rule, the most dependable support for landlords. The suburban streets of all cities could be lined with artistic homes similar to The Genessee with the money which is yearly fooled away with fakers who play upon the imagination of the inexperienced.

78

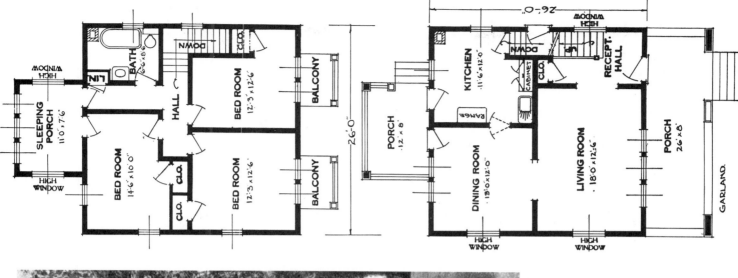

The GARLAND (Size 26x26')

The woman who knows that the surest way to a man's heart is through his sense of taste, and that sympathy and appreciation will lead him over mountains while criticism causes him to balk stubbornly on a level, can make any home an influence for permanent good whether it is of The Garland style of architecture or a more humble cottage.

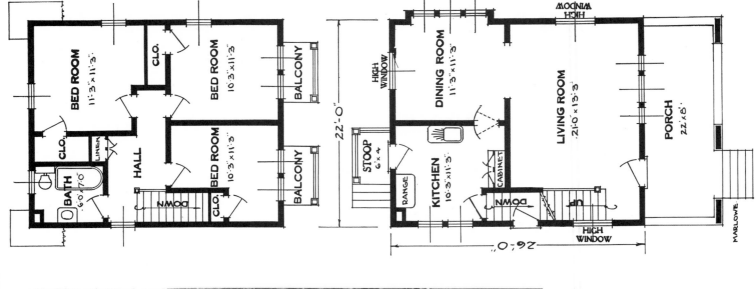

The MARLOWE (Size 22x26')

Men who would die for their wives, yet never bring in a pail of water or a scuttle of coal without grumbling, are seldom found in homes which have been built by mutual endeavor. Hands that help in making The Marlowe a home should gladly help in lightening the burdens of the helpmate whose kingdom lies within its threshold.

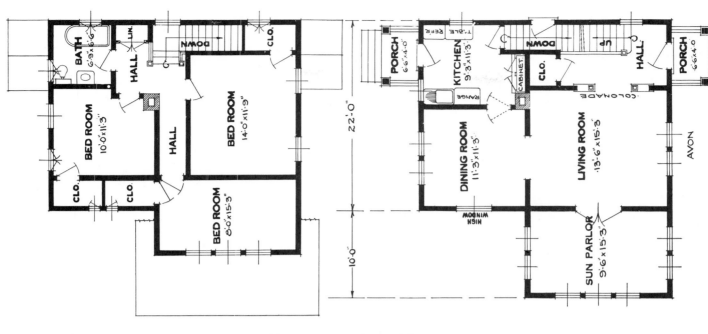

The AVON (Size 22x28')

Happiness was born a twin, and only he who seeks another's good, another's welfare, another's comfort can find his own. The man who early and wisely builds The Avon for a home for his family will not have to hunt for happiness elsewhere, for happiness is the product of good deeds and develops automatically within one's being.

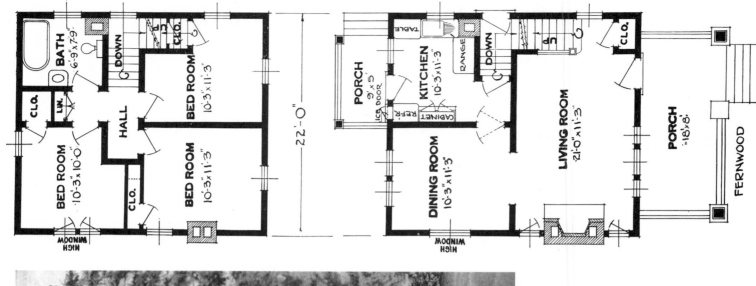

BED ROOM
10'-3"x10'-0"

BATH
6'-9"x7'-9"

CLO.

LIN.

CLO.

DOWN

UP

CLO.

HALL

BED ROOM
10'-3"x11'-3"

CLO.

BED ROOM
10'-3"x11'-3"

HIGH WINDOW

22'-0"

TABLE

PORCH
9'x5'

ICE DOOR

KITCHEN
10'-3"x11'-3"

RANGE

CABINET

REF.

DOWN

UP

CLO.

DINING ROOM
10'-3"x11'-3"

LIVING ROOM
21'-0"x11'-3"

PORCH
18'x8'

FERNWOOD

HIGH WINDOW

The FERNWOOD (Size 22x24')

Woman is by nature more economical than man, and her better judgment always offers protest against avoidable avenues of waste. To her rent receipts are constant reminders of funds foolishly spent, and constantly she sees a vision of a home, perhaps of The Fernwood style, which the rent money would shortly purchase.

82

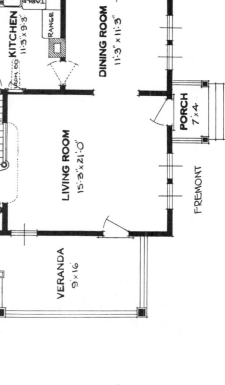

The FREMONT (Size 28x22')

In no other way can a man develop the respect of others for himself and his family as in the building of a home of his own. With home ownership comes fellowship and citizenship. One wins far more confidence by building a neat home on The Fremont plan, to meet his requirements, than in burdening himself and his wife with a larger house than is needed.

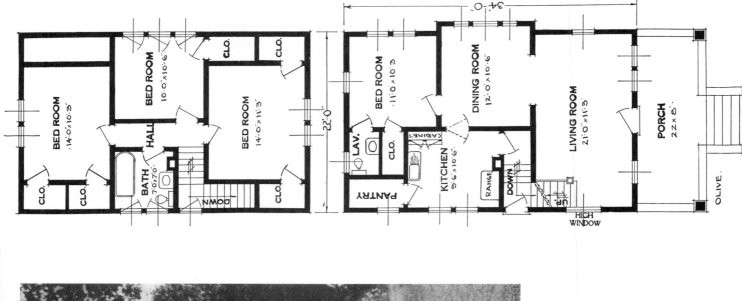

The OLIVE (Size 22x34')

Upon every face is written the record of the life the man or woman has lived and present thoughts and conditions are clearly shown in the voice and manner. Careworn faces and voices with discordant notes seldom emerge from happy new homes like The Olive, in which the very walls are respondent with mutual interest, sympathy, confidence and affection.

84

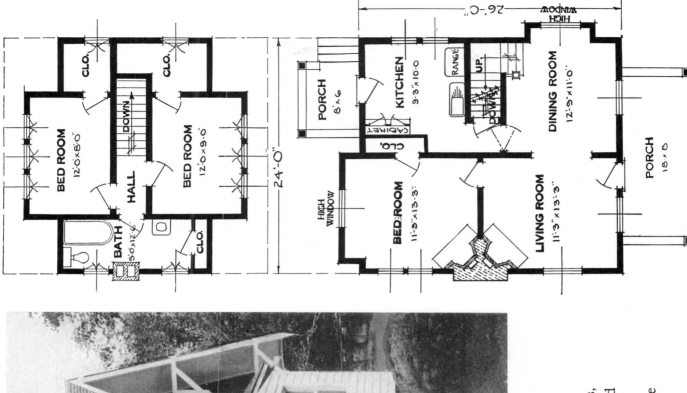

Floor plan labels (upper):

BED ROOM 12'-0"x8'-0" — CLO. — CLO. — DOWN — HALL — BED ROOM 12'-0"x9'-0" — BATH 5'-0"x12'-6" — CLO. — 24'-0"

26'-0" — HIGH WINDOW — PORCH 8'x6 — KITCHEN 9'-3"x10'-0" — RANGE — UP — DINING ROOM 12'-5"x11'-0" — CABINET — CLO. — DOWN — HIGH WINDOW — BED ROOM 11'-5"x13'-3" — LIVING ROOM 11'-5"x13'-3" — PORCH 18'x6 — LYNNHAVEN

The LYNNHAVEN (Size 24x26')

There is inestimable strength to be absorbed from foliage, trees and flowers, especially by those whose nature rebels at the thought of crowded halls and tenements.

For those who hunger for the wealth of inspiration which nature holds, The Lynnhaven will be found an ideal suburban home.

85

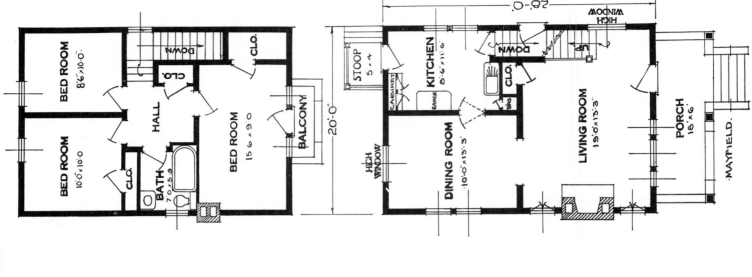

The MAYFIELD (Size 20x28')

It is not a question for a man to decide which he prefers to own five years later—a bundle of rent receipts or a substantial home like The Mayfield. The point to be decided is: where he wishes to build and what style of home. Any man can purchase a home on easy terms, who has the desire and determination to do so.

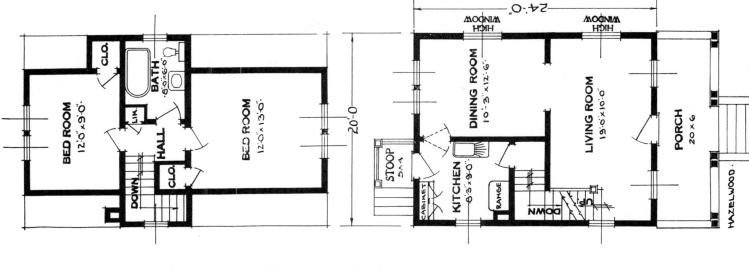

The HAZELWOOD (Size 20x24')

The money paid for rent will soon pay for the house rented, but it is still the landlord's, and the only thing of value which the renter has to show is a bundle of rent receipts. For those who resolve to spend their money more wisely, The Hazelwood will prove to be a permanent investment with daily dividends of independence beyond any monetary value.

87

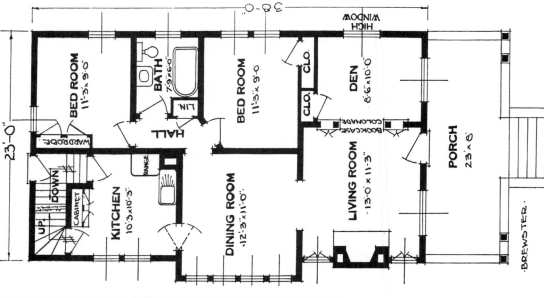

The nickels and dimes that go down in drink and up in smoke could easily solve the housing problem.

The BREWSTER (Size 23x38')

Forming a habit of placing in a Building and Loan Association all earnings which one does not need for immediate use is the surest road leading to the ownership of The Brewster for a home.

The sacrifices made in the saving of a home are the highly prized diary notes in one's record of accomplishment.

88

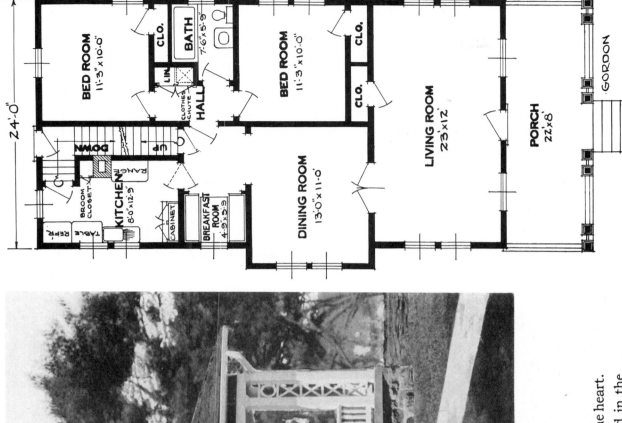

The GORDON (Size 24x44')

Keeping young is simply a question of keeping joy and sunshine in the heart. Age cannot furrow the heart which is daily, monthly and yearly bathed in the sunshine of conjugal peace. The sun never ceases to shine for those who constantly cultivate the spirit of calmness, kindness, courtesy, and cheerfulness in homes like The Gordon.

89

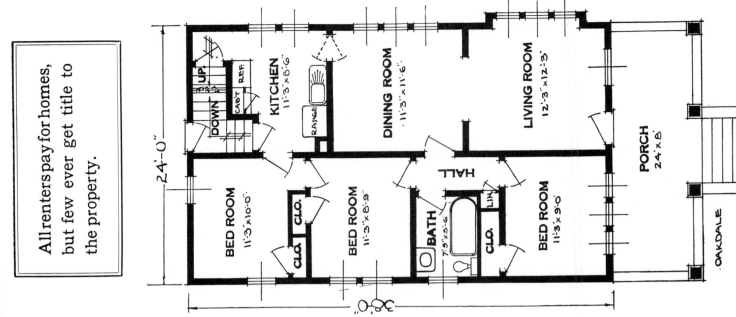

All renters pay for homes, but few ever get title to the property.

The OAKDALE (Size 24x38')

Had the laws of democracy been practiced in every land and country for the past ten centuries, such a thing as paying rent for a home would in this age be entirely out of the question. The unborn desire in every human heart for a home would at least prompt all to possess their place of habitation, even though it were not so beautiful as The Oakdale.

90

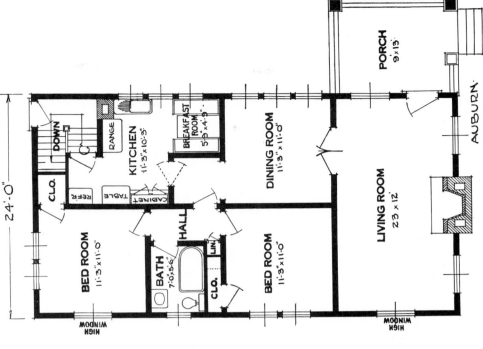

The AUBURN   (Size 24x44')

One takes little interest in beautifying a home and garden which belong to another, and which may be sold from under him without notice. There is a feeling of inappreciation and uncertainty which deeply affects his love for home. Those who build The Auburn, and know that every improvement added increases its value, will find both their time and money well and joyfully spent.

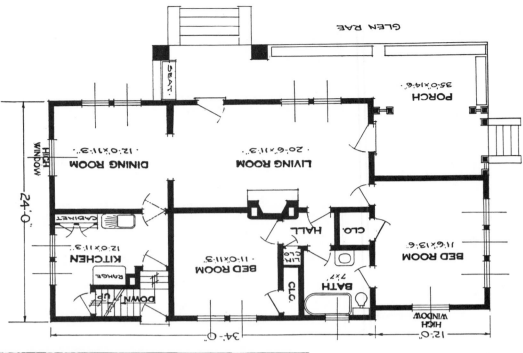

GLEN RAE

PORCH
35-0"x14-6"

DINING ROOM
12-0"x11-3"

LIVING ROOM
20-6"x11-3"

KITCHEN
12-0"x11-3"

BED ROOM
11-0"x11-3"

HALL

CLO.

BED ROOM
11-6"x13-6"

BATH
7x7

CABINET

RANGE

DOWN UP

SEAT

HIGH WINDOW

HIGH WINDOW

24'-0"

34'-0"

12'-0"

The GLEN RAE (Size 46x24')

Becoming dissatisfied with unpleasant and unsightly home surroundings is the sign of growth and possible strength necessary for advancement, and, if considered in this light rather than a complaint against fate, one should take courage and make greater effort, knowing that it is possible that The Glen Rae may soon become his home by the operation of the natural law of persistent purpose.

92

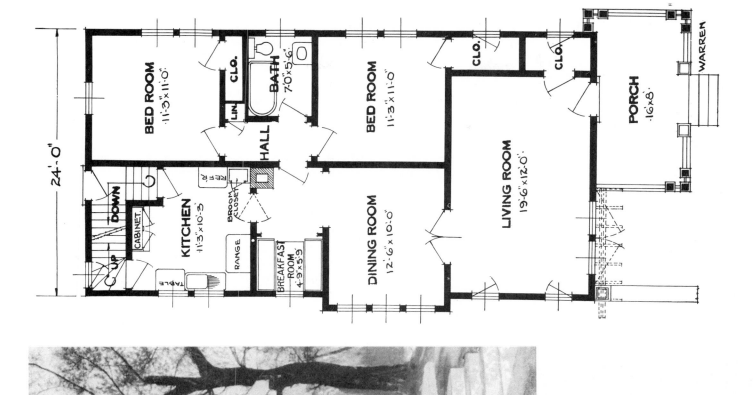

The WARREN (Size 24x44')

Now that reliable insurance companies in most of the states permit the basement garage without excessive insurance rates, many builders are taking advantage of the garage idea shown above. In addition to the convenience, and the saving in the initial cost, one's car is far better protected under all weather conditions, and its life is thereby materially lengthened.

93

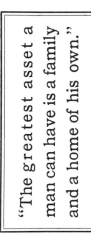

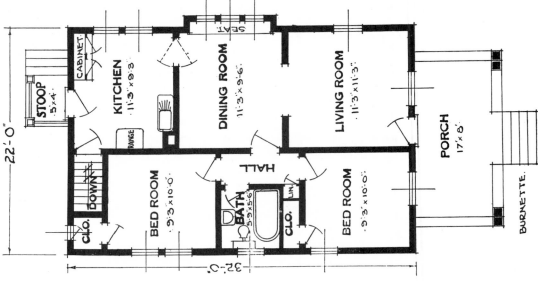

The BURNETTE (Size 22x32')

Crowded tenements and apartment houses are the hotbeds of jealousy, disease and discord. It is hard for the heart to find room for expression when the mind is full of the cobwebs of gossip. Those who are earnestly seeking a purer atmosphere, where their children can be brought up in a better environment, will find The Burnette an ideal house for a home.

94

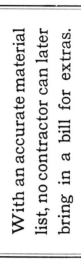

With an accurate material list, no contractor can later bring in a bill for extras.

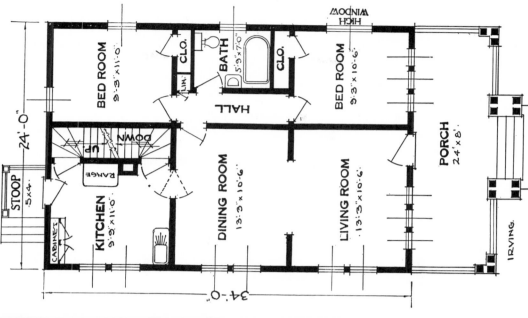

The IRVING (Size 24x34')

When a normal woman comes to herself at the age of twenty, twenty-two or twenty-four, according to her physical and mental growth, she realizes that her highest ambition is for a home of her own, affection and children, but her happiness is never complete until the love and home she wins is hers by all equitable and legal rights.

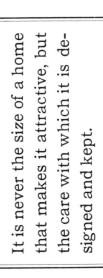

It is never the size of a home that makes it attractive, but the care with which it is designed and kept.

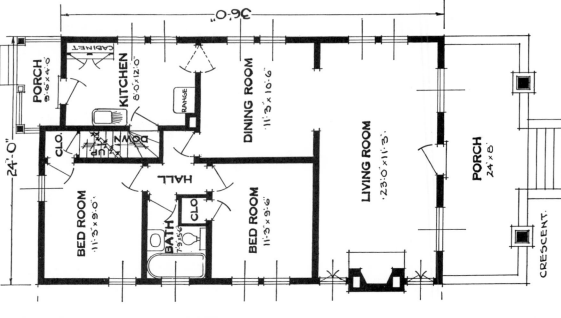

The CRESCENT (Size 24x36')

Practically all renters pay one-fourth of their earnings to landlords. This means that millions are monthly invested in worthless rent receipts. But this does not compare to the vast amount of home joy which the masses are missing. There is an inner joy and satisfaction in owning a convenient home of The Crescent plan which nothing else can give.

96

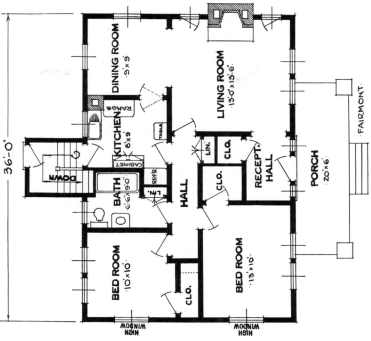

The happiest families are not those that rest in the lap of luxury, but rather those who express mutual sympathy in homes of simplicity.

The FAIRMONT (Size 36x24')

Hundreds of hearts yearn for a fuller, freer life in a beautiful little bungalow like The Fairmont. In small, convenient homes, life is longer, because there is less labor and the hearts are lighter. Dodging unnecessary drudgery in housework is simply applying twentieth-century efficiency methods to the business of housekeeping.

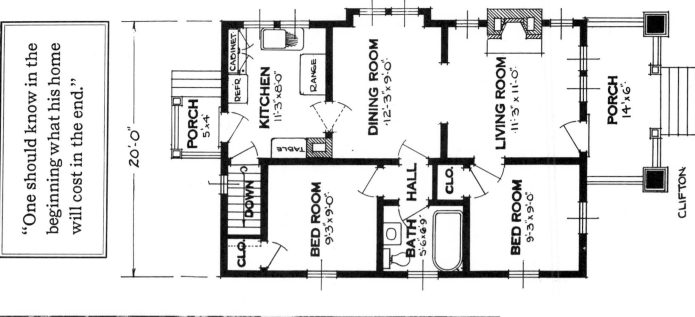

"One should know in the beginning what his home will cost in the end."

The CLIFTON (Size 22x30')

One of the greatest possible assets a man can plan and develop for the future safety of his wife and children is a home. If all men had the backbone and stamina to build for their family substantial homes similar to The Clifton, charitable institutions and orphan asylums would soon go out of business for the lack of inmates.

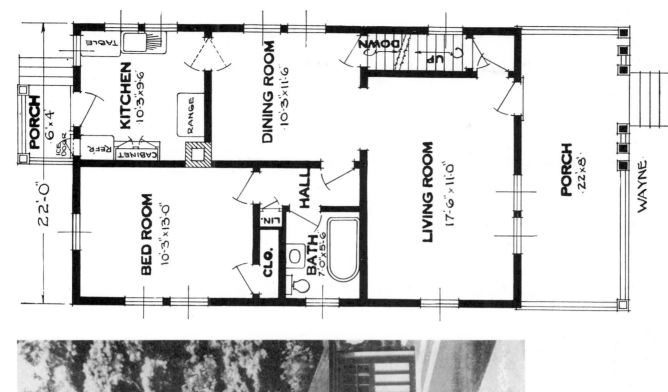

PORCH
6'x4'

22'-0"

KITCHEN
10'-3"x9'-6"

TABLE

RANGE

REFR.

CABINET

ICE DOOR

DINING ROOM
10'-3"x11'-6"

DOWN

UP

BED ROOM
10'-3"x13'-0"

CLO.

LIN.

BATH
7'-0"x5'-6"

HALL

LIVING ROOM
17'-6"x11'-0"

PORCH
22'x8'

WAYNE

The WAYNE (Size 22x34')

A good woman can make a cozy, comfortable home around any kind of a hearth, if her affections are satisfied. Single handed and alone, she cannot make the home joyful; she needs from her husband the multitudes of little courtesies and expressions of appreciation to which she is entitled. The Wayne is the style of home many women will delight in making happy.

99

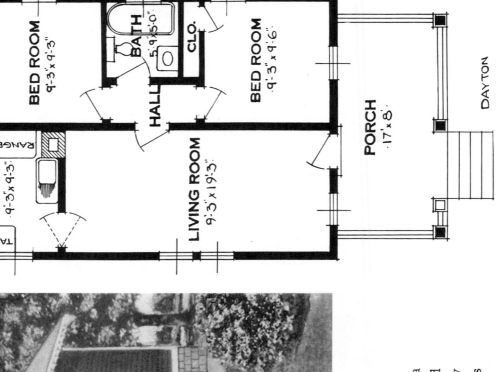

The DAYTON (Size 20x30')

The money one pays for rent is lost forever—it never comes back. It is a permanent investment which pays no dividends, and can never be converted into cash or exchanged for anything of value. When one's earnings are monthly invested in a neat home like The Dayton, he is soon enabled to realize his dreams for a home of his own.

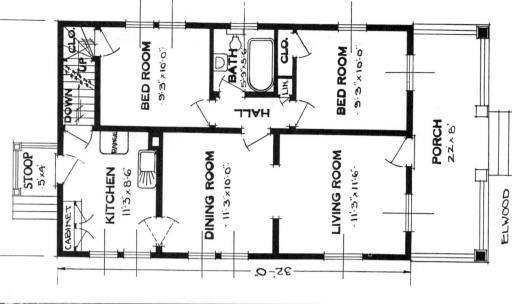

To build a house larger than is needed is a waste of money; and to care for it is a constant waste of toil and time.

The ELWOOD (Size 22x32')

It is when a man's earnings are paying for a home like The Elwood for himself and family that he is willing to work overtime and on holidays. There is a resolute note in his voice and a pride in his step seldom found in the man whose desire for a home has found no chance for expression in an undesirable and unsightly rented house.

The garage has become as essential a part of every home as the kitchen, and as a part of the Forrest it is an added attraction.

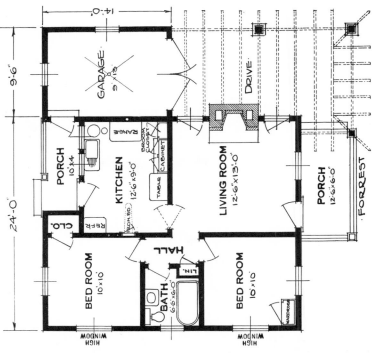

The FORREST (Size 24x28')

Large houses have caused thousands of industrious housewives to become prematurely old. The day for large, pretentious homes is rapidly passing, and the practice of economy in small, convenient homes like The Forrest is becoming the test of tactful wives. It is not the size of a home that makes it attractive, but the care with which it is kept.

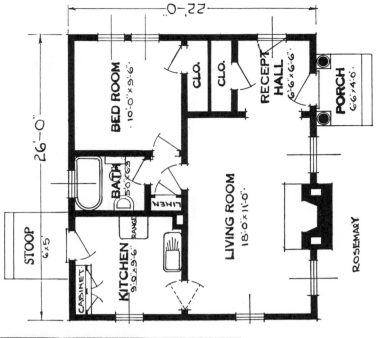

The ROSEMARY (Size 26x22')

All things beautiful are born of love—sometime, somewhere. The artist who fashioned The Rosemary must have been inspired by the influence of a kindred heart and yearned for a place of repose—a little kindgom of their own, far removed from the world of Commercialism where men clamor blindly for gold, and women are swayed by false flattery.

103

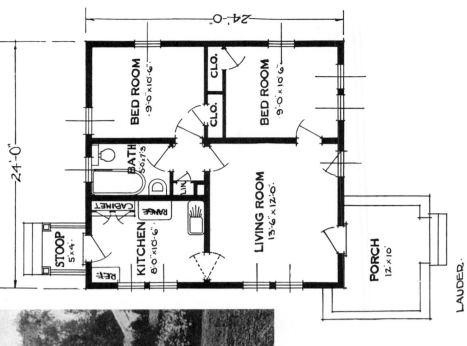

Floor plan labels:

- BED ROOM 9'-0"x10'-6"
- BED ROOM 9'-0"x10'-6"
- CLO.
- CLO.
- CLO.
- BATH 5'-0"x7'-3"
- KITCHEN 8'-0"x10'-6"
- RANGE
- CABINET
- REF.
- STOOP 5'x4'
- LIVING ROOM 13'-6"x12'-0"
- PORCH 12'x10'
- LAUDER.
- 24'-0"
- 24'-0"

The LAUDER (Size 24x24')

The feeling of aloneness is almost entirely unknown in small, comfortable homes like The Lauder. Mental depression comes, as a rule, from tired nerves and unsightly surroundings. In the small home which has been provided with an abundance of light, life is more cheerful and housekeeping is a pleasure, provided the husband daily expresses his appreciation.

104

Breakfast Room

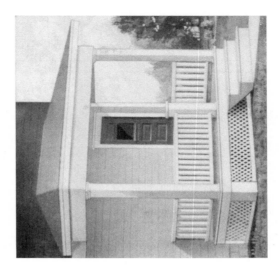

Addition No. 3

Addition No. 2

Addition No. 1

105

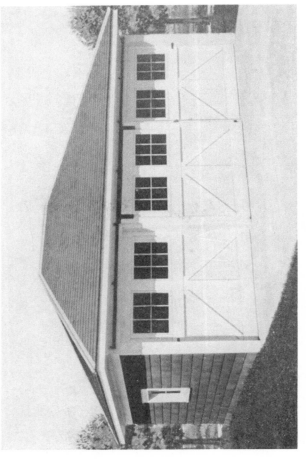

D-26

E-22

Complete Plans for any Garage $3

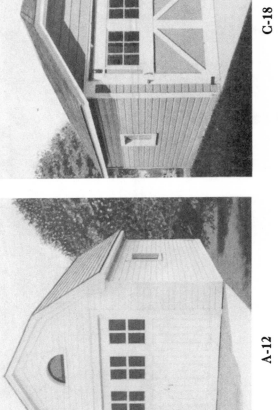

C-18

A-12

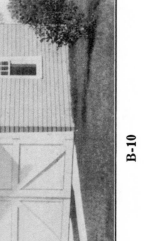

B-10

OUTSIDE DOORS

No. 7

No. 8

No. 5

No. 6

No. 3

No. 4

INSIDE DOORS

No. 1

No. 2

Home Ownership

The desire to own a home is one of the natural, primal instincts of every real man and woman. No other sentiment ever gets such a grip upon the human mind and heart as the vision of a home of one's own. It has been man's sublime incentive in all ages for greater effort. The basis of all his hopes and ambitions has ever been his dream of wife and child and home.

History is packed with the achievements of men who have been guided in their greatest efforts by this single star of hope—Home. Home is the sweetest word in human speech, and for the love and ownership of home, men have stood, without flinching, the hardest toil and torture that time and chance could bring upon them.

This picture of a home of love and peace has ever held the youth to his task and urged him onward and upward—through hardship and discouragement. It has ever been the source of inspiration for pure-minded women, and has enabled them to withstand the severest hardships gladly for the preservation of that which was to them more sacred even than life itself.

All Pay for a Home

No one can estimate what civilization owes to man's dream of a home of his own. The gratification of this deep-seated desire, and the toil and struggle and self-denial by which it is won, refines, elevates and ennobles. It inspires in men a self-respect which in turn inspires in others a respect for them—that makes them better men and better citizens, better husbands and better fathers. It gives them a standing and influence as freeholders in a community which nothing else can. Give every family a home of their own with lawn and garden and trees and flowers, and crime will disappear, and dishonorable deeds will become unknown.

Only about thirty-eight per cent of the American people own their own homes. The remaining sixty-two per cent are paying rent.

The money one pays to a landlord in exchange for rent receipts never comes back. It is a permanent investment which pays no dividends and can never be converted into cash or exchanged for anything of value.

Rent money will, in a few years, pay for the house rented, but the house still belongs to the landlord, and the only thing left in the possession of the renter is a bundle of rent receipts.

No family can ever acquire that deep-seated love and affection for a rented house which is naturally developed for a home they own. There is little incentive to adorn and beautify the house and lawn which belongs to another. But when the place which shelters the family group is their own—when they know that no man has a right to raise the rent or disturb their peace, then the place where they dwell, however lowly or humble it may be, becomes indeed their home. Every tree and shrub and flower planted adds new charm to life, and strengthens the ties that bind the happy hearts.

How Rent Money Counts Up

This table shows what rent amounts to in ten, fifteen and twenty years, with six per cent interest compounded annually, and gives an idea of the value of the house one can pay for by applying the rent-paying habit to the task of purchasing a home.

Rent per Month	In 10 Years	In 15 Years	In 20 Years
$ 10.00	$ 1,581.68	$ 2,793.10	$ 4,414.26
15.00	2,372.52	4,189.64	6,621.39
20.00	3,163.36	5,586.19	8,828.52
25.00	3,954.20	6,982.73	11,035.65
30.00	4,745.04	8,379.27	13,242.78
35.00	5,535.88	9,775.82	15,449.91
40.00	6,326.72	11,172.78	17,657.04
50.00	7,908.40	13,965.46	22,071.30
75.00	11,862.60	20,948.19	33,106.95
100.00	15,816.80	27,930.92	44,142.60

Ask for free booklet "How to Build and Finance Your Home."
This little book is helping thousands to solve their problems.

IMPORTANT

IN THIS collection of 101 Modern Homes is shown the greatest variety of designs ever offered in a single plan book, and each illustration has been produced from an actual photograph, and not from an artist's drawing.

Every home has been designed so that standard stock-length materials may be used without waste, and practically all windows and doors are of standard designs usually carried in stock.

It has required years to bring before the prospective home builder the hundreds of practical money-saving ideas to be found in this book, but the high cost of labor and building materials everywhere demanded just such a work.

Floor Plans

Every thoughtful home builder who studies carefully the great variety of floor plans shown will realize that every detail has been worked out for practical economy and convenience. Every window and door is located exactly as it should be to provide the right space for each piece of furniture, and every room has been provided with an abundance of light.

Changes in Floor Plans

While each floor plan has been especially and carefully arranged for each exterior design, yet it is entirely practical to make changes to meet the requirements of each builder, and any reliable contractor can easily move partition walls, windows or doors to suit the owner without affecting the exterior design to any great extent.

Kitchens

Large, cumbersome kitchens are no longer wanted by the modern efficient housewife who does her own work. Compact, time and step-saving kitchens are now demanded, and the floor plans shown herein conform in every detail to the most modern demands in this respect.

Breakfast Rooms

The greatest time-saving addition to the modern home is the Pullman Breakfast Room. While only about two-thirds of the homes illustrated show them, yet it is a very easy matter to arrange any kitchen so one may be added. (See illustration on page 105.)

Kitchen Fixtures

It is impossible to arrange all fixtures in all kitchens to suit all builders, but in the locations of sinks, ranges and cupboards, the watchwords have been convenience and economy. The location of any fixture, however, may be changed to meet the wishes of the builder.

Bathrooms

Attention is particularly called to the careful manner in which all bathrooms have been located and all fixtures arranged. By locating all bathrooms over kitchens a great saving is effected in the first cost, the upkeep is much reduced and all danger of damage to the walls of the best rooms by leaks or overflows is eliminated.

Blue Prints

The blue prints for each home have been prepared with the greatest possible care and when followed by the contractor there is not only a saving in construction of at least five to ten percent, but the exterior of the completed house is exactly as illustrated.

Blue prints and further details regarding any house furnished promptly.

Complete Standardized Plans that Save in the Cost of Construction

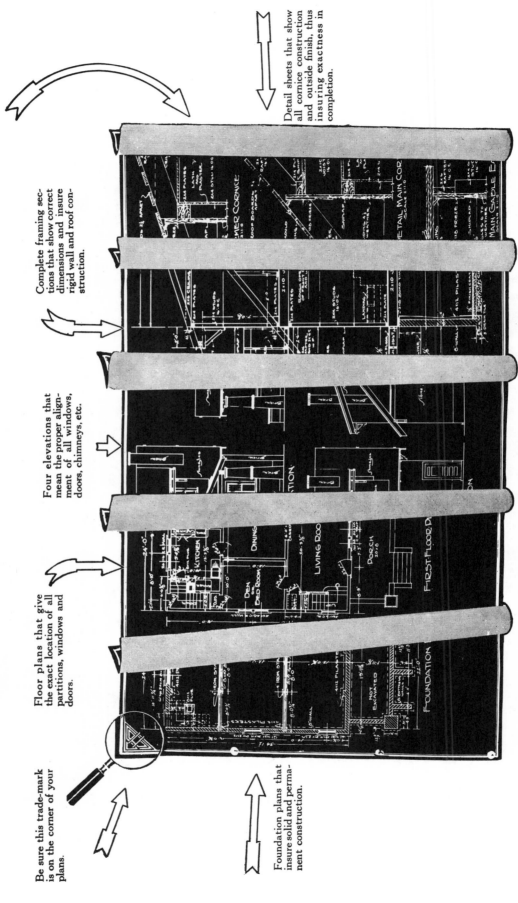

Detail sheets that show all cornice construction and outside finish, thus insuring exactness in completion.

Complete framing sections that show correct dimensions and insure rigid wall and roof construction.

Four elevations that mean the proper alignment of all windows, doors, chimneys, etc.

Floor plans that give the exact location of all partitions, windows and doors.

Be sure this trade-mark is on the corner of your plans.

Foundation plans that insure solid and permanent construction.

Regular size of stock plans 18 x 24 to 30, four to six sheets

Plans in duplicate (two sets), including specifications, furnished for any house in 24 to 48 hours for $——

This trade-mark on the corners of your house plans means that they are true copies of the original working plans for the homes shown in this plan book. The exterior of each house, when completed, will be exactly as illustrated if the plans are followed.

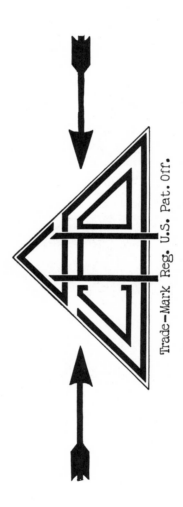

Trade—Mark Reg. U.S. Pat. Off.

Carefully standardized plans save labor, materials and time.

Reliable contractors invariably insist on complete plans so that satisfaction may be guaranteed.